GLAD TO BE A RESIDENT

Irreverent and Possibly Irritating Thoughts on
Anything by an Alien from an Old Country

W. JÜRGEN SCHRENK

iUniverse, Inc.
New York   Bloomington

iUniverse books may be ordered through booksellers or by contacting:

iUniverse
1663 Liberty Drive
Bloomington, IN 47403
www.iuniverse.com
1-800-Authors (1-800-288-4677)

ISBN: 978-1-4401-1216-4 (pbk)
ISBN: 978-1-4401-1217-1 (ebk)

Printed in the United States of America

iUniverse rev. date: 1/6/2009

CONTENTS[1]

[1] in alphabetical, to have at least some, order

PREFACE

In German, they are called "Nestbeschmutzer", i.e. birds who foul their own nest; Americans of a certain neck color simply tell them, "Love it or leave it". Both of course miss the point that love does not have to be blind, but should rather be tough. If you truly love your country, you should not hesitate (actually, feel obliged) to criticize her perceived flaws and make every effort towards further improvement. A famous person (not a celebrity) once said something to the effect that "The US are an all screwed-up country, but the best there is", which comes pretty close to my own evaluation. That is why a planned 2-year postdoctoral stay turned into a life-long love affair, but why I also dare to draw unfavorable comparisons every now and then. Some might find this objectionable and prefer to proclaim the United States to be the greatest country in the world – often without much to compare it to, as they have rarely spent a significant amount of time traveling abroad. In fact, the most ardent protagonists of the superlative often don't even know their own country very well.

There is much to love in America (although there may have been more in the past and hopefully be again in the future), and Germany - while an old country - is certainly a good one, too, albeit far from perfect. Having lived in both for more than thirty years (Yes, I am that old), I could not help but make critical observations regarding the different strengths and weaknesses, and the communalities based on the fact that Germans and Americans are above all both human and prone to perpetuating inherited errors as well as to adding new mistakes as we go along.

The purpose of writing down some of the impressions collected over many years is not to tick everybody off (although that may well be the unfortunate result), but to make the reader pause, think, and consider changes for the better, which is probably a sign of naive immaturity on my side. Since there seems to be little harm in trying, however, here you go.

N.B.: In the following chapters, "Americans", "Germans", etc. usually means "many", sometimes "most", never "all". Generalizations are generally wrong, except for this one, of course. 300 million Americans and 80 million Germans cover a broad spectrum of individuals. So you, Dear Reader, can rest assured that you are not included in any unfavorable description.

Acknowledgments
To avoid the accusation of plagiarism, I explicitly thank Al Gore for his inconvenient truth, Sarah Palin for the many gems she produced during her time in the national limelight (hockey mom, Joe Sixpack, pitbull with lipstick), and John McCain for Joe the Plumber.

A Young Country

The United States are too diverse to permit an easy classification under one headline, but if I had to try, I would characterize her as an adolescent nation. A couple of centuries don't amount to much in the history of countries, and the US seem to have grown too fast to truly appreciate and put to good use her supreme power.

She has now reached an important decision point and will have to make up her mind over the next few decades. Does she want to be the home of reckless Wild West-style strongmen (and women), who think the world's problems are best solved with big guns, or become a sophisticated player guiding less advanced ones to the High Road she claims to be pursuing? With hunting, fishing and hockey as pleasant recreational activities, but not as the highest and most appealing goal in life.

The Founding Fathers would have a strong recommendation, but does anybody still listen?

AFRICA

Africa is not only one of the most beautiful and interesting parts of this world, but also plagued by some of its biggest problems: Warfare of unimaginable cruelty, widespread starvation, horrific frequency of infectious and often incurable diseases, and a lack of resources to address these issues. If you ignore the nonsensical ideological solution proposed by America's know-it-all Scientist-in-Chief a.k.a. President, you are faced with a most inconvenient truth.

First of all, Africa is a continent populated way over its carrying capacity – an ecological term defining the number of living beings a given area can support. A continent with vast deserts and the corresponding climate just cannot accommodate an ever-growing population, even if they devour all their bush meat and burn their remaining forests for agriculture and fuel. Sorry, Mr. President, but the answer to this is not celibacy (which does not even work to prevent extramarital affairs of married members of this administration), but education and contraception. Well-intended rules don't help – remember, you could not even keep your own daughters out of trouble with the law.

So provide Africa with true humanitarian aid: Realistic means to control its population growth, hands-on advice how to develop local economies based on renewable resources, and help to combat the present flood of diseases from AIDS to tuberculosis to malaria.

Mosquito netting, condoms and affordable drugs are urgently needed to cure the causes, not just treat the symptoms of today's problems – as well as orphanages for the many thousand children robbed of their parents by the still rampant scourge of AIDS.

And save the pious and bigot lecturing for better days…

AMERICAN CARS

I do feel sorry for the thousands of workers in the American Auto industry, who have already lost their jobs or are going to loose it. The present problems in this industry are not their fault, and certainly also not the result of "unfair competition", as is claimed by the industry's lobbyists with their deep pockets and the compliant members of Congress. Solely to blame are the complacent and incompetent executives of American car companies, who for decades ignored warning signs (Remember the oil crisis in the late seventies?) and the success of the Japanese imports, and collected huge bonuses for being asleep at the wheel..

When we came to this country in 1972, we brought our little FIAT with us – big mistake. Not just because it was a FIAT and then – a friend of ours brought her Audi with her recently and suffered a similar fate, The DMV calls your 4-wheeled companion a "gray market car" and can (and will!) make your life miserable for months to come. We were lucky enough eventually to find a rational and compassionate DOT person of authority, who decided that our little car would not be a danger on American roads, although it lacked an obviously essential buzzer that could not be retrofitted.

After this harrowing experience, we decided to buy American – a "sport sedan" and a mobile home conversion van. Both soon displayed signs of shoddy workmanship and cost us almost as much in repairs as the original purchase price, and so like many Americans we then went Japanese. As an aside: When we bought our son his first car in 1994, we ignored our past bad experience and selected an American car again – even from the same family as our two lemons. (What the heck – I am talking Chrysler, Dodge and Plymouth.) It was fun to drive (We were allowed to borrow it, when it needed new tires) and as reliable as it could be – so there was progress.

Being old and German, we finally moved up from our Japanese sedan (not as problem-free as its manufacturer claimed) to the first Mercedes in our lives and love it. We are still driving our 8 year-old Japanese 4-WD, as it has carried us faithfully even over ridge roads in the Mexican border area that our Border Patrol "pilot" said he was scared to drive. Our next 4-WD, however, may well be an American car again – I know the engineering capability and experience is there, and if those executives have finally learnt their lesson, we might even be able to afford the gas.

BALANCE

Statistics show (and my own experience confirms) that Americans work longer hours and have less vacation time than nationals of any other industrialized country. Consequently, they enjoy a higher standard of living than anybody else, as measured by the number and size of cars, TVs, other toys, and even houses.

Amazingly, Germans and most other Europeans don't seem to get that this is the most desirable goal of all. Again and again, in polls German and other European workers prefer more leisure time over wage increases, if they have to choose one (Both of course would be best) - why?

One reason is the frequently cited need "to recharge your batteries". No matter how much you love your work – if it includes periods of stress (and all attractive jobs do), then you simply need time off occasionally. One of my favorite past coworkers, a workaholic scientist, prided himself of not having taken a vacation for many years, while his colleagues including myself could not help but notice unmistakable changes in his usually pleasant personality. I literally had to force him to take a vacation (by locking him out of our high security research building), which he reluctantly decided to spend on a house boat reading scientific papers, fishing and drinking beer. He came back his old pleasant self, full of energy and eager to get back to work, and has turned this experience into an annual ritual ever since.

Another reason is the realization that postponing non-work-related pleasures until you are retired is a gamble you don't really want to take. Your health may no longer be up to what you always wanted to do – or you may simply drop dead three months after your farewell party, just when you were going to rent the RV to finally see Grand Canyon. At a time when immediate gratification is expected by almost everyone, it is astonishing how many people delay the fulfillment of a life's dream until their "Golden Years", which unfortunately may turn out not to be that golden after all.

A while back I ran into a former high-powered marketing executive and colleague of mine, whom we had taken years earlier on a day trip to see thousands of migrating Sandhill Cranes – a nature experience to behold, but of which we are fortunate enough to have had many during our regular weekend trips and vacations. He, however, remembered that day as one of the most beautiful he had ever experienced, told me how he regretted not to have more of these memories, and how important it is to lead a balanced life. He realized that after a stellar career, during which he focused all his energy on turning his life-long employer into one of the most successful companies in the industry while completely neglecting his personal life. By now "his company" has been acquired by an even bigger one, making him dispensable, his wife had tragically died an early death, and he is faced with a Gains & Losses statement that leaves him very unhappy.

So keep that Australian advice in mind, "Work hard and play hard", and don't postpone the play until after the work. There may just not be any time left, and "He (or she) who dies with the most toys wins" may not be the most rewarding bottom line after all.

Remember instead that we are not termites with one single purpose in life – but that being human includes a well-rounded personality as the result of a balanced lifestyle. Work is important and much of the time rewarding, but other components of our lives are equally essential and should be indispensable. Humans need good music (classical, folk, jazz) to play or at least listen to, art from paintings to architecture to create or enjoy in galleries, museums or historic sites, and any other means to stay in touch with and internalize the great cultural accomplishments mankind has achieved over the centuries.

Just as important is never to loose the connection with nature and the environment of which we are part, but to enjoy it consciously the Thoreau and Muir way. Checking off natural wonders (Been there, done that), listing bird species pointed out by a professional guide and similar activities miss the point, but even a modest stroll in the woods or tending your garden are right on the mark. Learning a little about geology, astronomy and the likes also helps with the perspective to see us humans and our role in the right place in time and space. As a result, you will find it easy to be happy and content most of the time, and might even feel stimulated to contribute to fields outside your immediate profession. You won't be in danger to turn into a fanatic crusader of religious, political, health or other issues, and when your time is up, you won't feel regrets or remorse about having missed out on anything important to you.

BASIC EDUCATION

If you read the results of polls attempting to investigate the level of education of the general public, some of the numbers are hard to believe. If they are indeed true, then 20 % of Americans assume the sun revolves around the earth. !5 % cannot find the United States on a world map, 8 % do not know that Alaska is a state of the Union but assume it is a territory or foreign nation (That may have changed recently), 13 % do not agree that plants produce the oxygen that makes our atmosphere breathable, and 24 % don't think that light travels faster than sound. And yes, a staggering 50 % do not "believe" in evolution, including three former Republican presidential candidates, who fortunately dropped early out of the Primary race.

(The term "believe" was incorrectly used in the original question – like gravity, evolution is not a matter of belief, but of having been taught at least some basic facts of biology, paleontology and anthropology. Which may reflect the sad reality that 8 % of High School biology teachers instruct their students that "Intelligent Design" is a valid alternative to Darwin's theory of evolution. The outgoing President of the United States may have had the bad fortune of being victimized by one of these teachers.)

It is on this background that even California, one of the more progressive states of the nation, is planning to slash its educational budget by 10 %, virtually guaranteeing that America's superb universities not withstanding, the elementary education will have no chance ever to catch up with that in for instance Southeast Asian countries, which seem to have discovered that bright children trained by well-educated teachers are their future. Of course good education is no guarantee for success – as they say, it provides you with the software; what you do with it, is up to you. But it sure helps to have a running start.

Now compare this rather sad picture of our educational level with the statistics that 91 % of American households own at least one bible, with an average of four (4). This great book has been the top bestseller every year in recent history; in 2005 alone Americans bought 25 million bibles – and 47 % of Americans claim to read in it every week.

Please don't get me wrong – there is absolutely no conflict between being religious AND well-educated. In fact, many outstanding scientists (some of whom I have had the pleasure to meet personally) are devout Christians, Moslems, Hindus, you name it – and clerics of all major denominations have no problem coming to an agreement between their faith and scientific evidence. What is required for that, however, is a fundamental understanding of both fields: knowing at least a few scientific facts, and reading the bible as it is meant to be read. Remember when it was written, by whom and for which readership (For an eternal God, a few billion years would be like a week for us mortals, and by taking the Good Book verbatim, you are placing yourself on the intellectual and educational level of fishermen 2,000 years ago.).

Then it will be easy to answer the question, what would require a more intelligent designer: building fossils as well as existing organisms from clay, or designing the grand scheme of evolution and planting the seeds for it? Once that is resolved, even an occasional popular science publication might find its way onto American book shelves. And I won't have to feel sorry any longer for all the people missing out completely on many of mankind's great cultural achievements in the sciences from biology to cosmology, but who still voice strong opinions on topics they know very little or nothing about.

That is only the science part of basic education. Once you start looking at arts from music to painting, the picture tends to be just as bleak. And languages? I have actually heard talk show hosts state that teaching and learning foreign languages is unpatriotic, including the Spanish and French spoken by America's neighbors. How uneducated can one be and take pride in it?

On the other hand, you can be president and control much of the world's nuclear arsenal without being able to even pronounce the word correctly, or become his spokesperson without ever having heard of the Cuban missile crisis. You can ignore evolution and believe in Intelligent Design, or in ghosts (half the American people do according to polls; + 3 %?), and still qualify for the highest office. So why bother with basic education? This is the country of unlimited opportunity, provided you have the right daddy with the necessary connections.

Behaving like an Animal

It has always eluded me why one of the more serious insults to a human being is calling him/her an animal, often reserved for perpetrators of particularly heinous crimes. The vast majority of animal species and their individual members live fairly exemplary lives in accordance with most American community standards. They take care of their offspring with complete dedication, often ready even for the ultimate sacrifice to protect them (No child abuse here). They eat what they need (Obesity is not a problem), and if they are predators, swiftly kill to eat (Torturing victims is usually not part of the game). They have sex to procreate and occasionally for fun, and readily accept the consequences (Abortions not necessary). Most are clean and spend an appropriate amount of time preening to stay that way, but otherwise accept their natural look (Cosmetics are unheard of). They age with dignity, are highly respected because of their accumulated experience and often lead the group – silverback gorillas and mature female elephants, for instance (No need for Botox injections or implants in an attempt to gain acceptance or postpone the inevitable). Overall, they do what comes naturally, leaving them most of the time healthy, social and in balance with their environment. Which makes me wonder, who (if anybody) should feel insulted, if you call a human an animal.

Interestingly, in German the word "*tierisch*" (animal-like) is almost exclusively used in connection with "*Ernst*" (seriousness). During the carnival season, each year a medal is given to celebrities who have shown a sense of humor in their public lives, the "*Orden wider den tierischen Ernst*" . Which would suggest that at least Germans consider a salient feature of humanity the ability to make fun of institutions, customs and - most important - oneself.

So before getting too upset about the idea of behaving like an animal with a sense of humor, imagine what the widespread implementation of this behavior would do for our society and many of its problems...

Being Alone

There is a big difference between being alone and being lonely. Nobody likes the latter, but quite a few people including myself need to be by themselves every now and then. It allows to think, daydream, make plans, evaluate situations, recharge the proverbial batteries – in short, just plain sort through things and events.

On the other hand, there are more and more fellow human beings, who seem to be afraid of quiet hours. They need continuous action, socializing, multitasking and distractions of all kinds. If "nothing is happening", they rather organize a spontaneous party with like-minded friends than being faced with solitude.

If the trend continues, society stands a good chance of becoming a maelstrom of busybodies with not much time for individual development and cultural progress. Instead, crisis management and dashing madly from one urgent task to the next will fill the day, interrupted only by text messaging or e-mailing your fellow ant hill residents.

Sometimes it feels really good to be old enough to be called so twentieth-century.

BIG PHARMA

Second only to Big Oil, Big Pharma is one of consumers' and their advocates' favorite targets. How can the same brand-name drug cost much less in Canada or Mexico, and why are generics even cheaper, if not because of the unbridled greed of those reckless healthcare companies? The true answer is quite a bit more complex than this.

For the sake of argument, let's assume, the manufacturing, packaging and distribution of a medicine costs about 10¢ per dose, and yet you are charged 1$ for it. The reason? While the optimized high-throughput manufacturing of a drug can often be dirt cheap, its discovery, development and clinical trials were hugely expensive, and during the time it is protected by a patent (around 20 years), the company has to recover these costs as well as those for drugs which never made it to the market due to problems that arose late in the game, often during its final trials. Generics manufacturers of course do not have these expenses – they can wait until the patent protection expires and then sell the same pill for 30¢ at a 200% profit. This generic product *if made in the US,* by the way, underlies the same stringent control by the FDA as the original and is just as good. In fact, quite a few big pharmaceutical companies sell their original medications also in a different package under a generic name. That won't help to recover the hundreds of millions of sunken development costs, but at least contribute a bit to the bottom line.

For a similar reason, companies sell their original products in certain countries for less than in the US – because those countries' governments control the price, and if you don't comply, you cannot sell anything. Again, a smaller profit is better than none.

Big Pharma's argument therefore is simple: If their original drugs would have to be sold everywhere at lower prices, there just would not be enough left to finance the development of newer and better medications, period. That of course is not completely honest, either, as the profit margins of bestselling drugs are well padded and could be slimmed down quite a bit without putting their producers in financial jeopardy.

So don't feel bad about buying your supplies across the border or switching to generics altogether; you are not going to ruin a charitable organization. One word of caution, however: Not all generics are what the seller promises, and pretty bad or even outright dangerous stuff can be bought over the Internet or from murky sources, more often than not in Southeast Asia. So even while holding on to your wallet, make sure you obtain legitimate products.

BIOFUEL

In the past, quite a few chemists claimed that the dumbest thing you could do with oil is to burn it, since it is an ample but finite natural resource containing numerous valuable organic compounds of great potential utility for other applications. In the resulting sensible search for alternative sources of fuel, we now managed to take stupidity even one step further and came up with the idea that burning food for an increasingly hungry world would be an intelligent solution.

Brazil showed the way by demonstrating nearly complete independence from oil through mass production of ethanol from sugar cane, feasible and cost-effective. Even the impact on food supply is negligible – how much cachaça can you consume. The true price paid will become obvious later, when the destruction of vast areas of the planet's largest rainforest for the sake of huge cane fields and its consequences for the local climate and the world's biodiversity can no longer be ignored.

Worse still at least in the short term, however, are the copy-cat attempts by Europe and North America, whose temperate climate and more limited space for agriculture do not allow seas of sugar cane. Instead, anything from corn and wheat to soybeans, sunflowers and rape seed is converted to ethanol, at great expense but attractive to farmers due to generous subsidies by short-sighted governments. Who cares that as a result staple foods for the poorest in the world become unaffordable, as politicians in the industrial countries bask in the comfort of acting "green".

And this is not even the end of the line: Cash-strapped entrepreneurs and profit-maximizing corporations have discovered that palm oil is a cheaper fuel to burn. So after the Amazon, the earth's second largest rain forest in Indonesia is slashed and burnt to give way to more monocultures, with similar consequences for climate and biodiversity.

All this is happening, while more and more people are concerned about global warming (Can you imagine, what burning huge areas of oxygen-producing forests does to the CO_2-level in our atmosphere?). And while cutting-edge technologies from growing algae in fermenters to harnessing solar energy more effectively are pursued by research institutions and small companies with meager funds at the same time, when oil companies in the US receive tax breaks to drill for more oil (preferably in protected areas) and farmers in Europe are better off selling their produce for fuel production rather than food.

Will science, technology and just plain common sense ever influence politics before it is too late?

BIPARTISANSHIP

I find it difficult to understand, why everybody in Washington talks about it, but very few members of Congress actually practice it. No matter how strong your position may be on key issues, there is always enough overlap to accomplish at least something (other than blaming your opponents for not being cooperative).

I think hunting other than subsistence hunting is atavistic, and who loves shooting should practice it in a target range without killing animals. I also have limited understanding for the joy of tearing up the desert or coastal dunes with ATVs and in the process destroying fragile plant life. And yet I am ready to form a coalition with hunters or off-roaders any time, when it comes to protecting open space from urban sprawl or other development. What to do with the saved spaces is then topic for later discussions and negotiations.

This is what bipartisanship should look like. Wherever you come from and wherever you want to end up eventually, join forces and go part of the way together. This gives you more clout, increases your chances of success, and – along the way – may help you to understand "the other side" enough to identify future opportunities of working together.

If tree-hugging environmentalists can do that, why is the entrenched Washington establishment so inflexible?

BIRDWATCHERS

When we first moved to this country, birdwatching was a hobby for old ladies in tennis shoes, and younger people with binoculars tended to attract the attention of the local police. Germany was not much different, and I recall vividly being chased as a Peeping Tom by a bunch of nudists enjoying the sun right next to a Common Tern colony on the banks of the Isar river south of Munich.

Just a few decades later, nearly half the Americans claim birdwatching as their hobby (although many of them can't tell a swan from a goose or a heron from a crane), and the formerly innocent pastime has turned into a billion dollar industry. Whole specialty stores offer everything from bins (the insider short form for binoculars) to tape recorders to multi-pocket jackets, field guides to the birds of remote parts of the world and software to manage your life list. Birders (as they are now called) use terms like "ticks", "lifers" and "peeps" only obvious to the initiated, and lengthy names are abbreviated to TV (Turkey Vulture, not television) or whooper. Not to be outdone, particularly creative German *ornis* have even come up with *Sossel, Mossel* and *Wossel* (for the admittedly cumbersome *Singdrossel, Misteldrossel* and *Wacholderdrossel*) to facilitate swift communication with fellow enthusiasts.

Worldwide the birding community has split into two markedly different camps. There are the old-fashioned birdwatchers, who enjoy observing even familiar backyard species at length and in great detail just like any other nature lover. And then there are the listers, whose main purpose in life is checking off as many species as possible. They maintain county, state and country lists and brag about how many species they have seen in a "Big Day" or in one year. They go through great expense to lengthen their checklist by joining organized groups, whose guides lure even the shyest birds into visibility by playing their songs off a tape or disc. Economic listers decide on their next travel destination based on the calculation how many potential new species they can expect to see per money spent, and don't waste time on watching a bird once it is identified (by their leader) and checked off on their list. The lucky few, who have reached the upper echelon of listers (let's say, 6,000+ species) and the financial resources, won't mind spending a small fortune on further adorning their standing and will jet to Maine on short notice to add that vagrant Ross's Gull to their US life list (anybody can see it in Churchill) or to Minnesota for a Fieldfare. True love and appreciation of nature is not involved – they might as well collect baseball cards or beer mats (If it were as fashionable as birding, they probably would.). Nothing to spurn of course – already Goethe observed that collectors are happy people.

Of course seeing a "lifer" (i.e. a particular kind of bird for the first time in your life) is exciting also to a traditional naturalist, whether he or she keeps a life list or not. I find it to be more fun though, if it happens unexpectedly during a hike or nature walk rather than pointed out by a professional guide as one of the "target species" on an organized trip. Then any bird becomes a "good" one, a classification reserved by listers for uncommon species.

No matter how bizarre some of the birding excesses might seem to the outsider, the overall impact of this fad is fortunately beneficial not only for the economy but also the environment (the occasional trampling of a rare bird by overeager observers not withstanding). Endangered species and dwindling habitats receive better protection because of their importance in attracting visitors, and local communities in developing countries benefit directly from ecotourism. Even old-fashioned birdwatchers can still enjoy their feathered friends, as long as they manage to avoid the busloads of telescope-wielding fans. As a welcome fringe benefit, areas attractive to rare birds and therefore to birders more often than not harbor other animals and plants not commonly seen elsewhere, thus rewarding the observant visitor even if the birds prove elusive. You may then come back from your first visit to Costa Rica with only 185 bird species jotted down in your note book rather than with 365 after a guided tour, but with a much deeper appreciation for the rainforest and better understanding of its conservation needs.

As an additional reward, you may every now and then discover something truly new, highly unlikely if you limit your explorations to the paths well beaten by countless predecessors. Whether then anybody believes you, is a different matter, but who cares. My Buff-collared Nightjar on a Mexican Island, one of the last Nukupuus on Kauai, or the Whooping Crane by a Texas farm road were equally exciting, believable or not.

BUGS

One of the things Americans fear most in life are bugs – bugs not in the biological sense (Hemiptera), but defined as everything from virus and microorganisms ("germs") to insects and other arthropods. This is the reason why Americans have discovered the pleasures of outdoor dining and sidewalk cafés that late (or often not yet), and preferably only in a city environment with few or no flying and buzzing creatures around. Notable exception is the long-standing tradition of barbecuing, which – if properly practiced -, however, creates enough smoke to keep any reasonable insect at a safe distance anyway. Just to make sure, a multitude of additional precautions are usually met, from old-fashioned citronella candles to electric bug zappers to high-tech electronic devices. Nevertheless, I have frequently heard people scream or seen them take flight upon the sighting of an innocent moth or bee approaching an outdoors congregation, until a courageous soul chased the threat away or heroically swatted it.

These phobias (germo- and others) are of course a blessing not only for the makers of camping accessories, but also for the producers of many other consumer items. The ideal household is kept all but sterile through the highly recommended (i.e. advertised) use of germicidal sponges, wipes, hand soaps, air fresheners and so on, and should not be contaminated by unfiltered water, food items not purchased in a supermarket, etc. Naturally, there is an exception to this rule, too: pets. Man's/Woman's best friend, for instance, is welcome to lick his owner's face, and what could show more affection than a kiss right after Fluffy has sampled other dogs' poop in the street.

In the filthy Old World, on the other hand, most people are oblivious towards the dangers lurking in the disguise of flying bugs. They nonchalantly sit in a Trattoria and seem to ignore the occasional moth burning up in the flame of the candle decorating the table, or committing suicide in its molten wax. And on a warm summer afternoon, careless Bavarians relax in a beergarden under old chestnut trees with the only protection against swarms of wasps provided by a half-full glass of beer sitting on the handrail, to attract and drown the invaders. Untrained by educational marketing as they are, these same people keep their homes simply clean not decontaminated, but incoherently don't allow their pets to lick their faces.

Obviously, much common sense still needs to be acquired here or there. Possibly this could be bad for the economy, but good for the immune system – and for the efficacy of established overused antibiotics.

CELEBRITIES

It used to be that you became famous for outstanding accomplishments in any field of interest to the world – arts, science, sports, finance, warfare, you name it. Showing your private parts in public was not sufficient.

That has obviously changed, since you can be a modern celebrity (celeb, as they are called affectionately) without any merits other than having been born to rich or famous parents, or having behaved particularly scandalously at a widely publicized function. This will secure you continuous media coverage (thanks to modern technology with almost instantaneous worldwide distribution) and the lasting gratitude of a faithful fan club. With little additional effort, you should also soon be hosting your own talk show on television or satellite radio, especially if you continue to behave irrationally in the presence of reporters or – if you have already progressed that far - your own entourage of paparazzi. Other than being a celebrity, no qualification seems to be necessary, although a run-in with the law is certainly helpful.

Don't blame the media for the appalling state of affairs, though. Most have long given up any ambition to be educational, but feed the audience whatever will result in the highest ratings, to attract more advertisers. The latter of course try to use celebrities whenever possible such as former sports stars or actors no longer willing or able to seriously act. So the never-ending circle continues and everybody is happy, including the increasing number of rubber-necking viewers, who have missed out on getting a life. They may continue to dream of their own five minutes in the limelight, maybe as participants in a reality show or eyewitnesses interviewed on local TV. If such an opportunity eludes you, you can still impress people by name-dropping. Just make sure you don't sound like a groupie, but only use first names as if you were a best friend.

So what about the people who were famous for a good reason? They still exist, jealously guard their privacy and rarely show up in the news. Deservedly so, as they are a boring lot nobody cares about. Like, you know, stuff they tried to teach you in high school, you know. Like stuff, you know, that really doesn't matter any more, you know.

Interestingly, the only profession where rock-star-status is undesirable seems to be that of President of the United States. He is instead expected to trigger protests and demonstrations wherever he still dares to travel, and a candidate who doesn't must be unqualified for the highest office. That limitation does not apply to a female candidate for vice presidency, for whom rock star status is a plus. You betcha.

CHANGE

"Change" and "Hope" are heavily used words these days, initially employed by one of the presidential hopefuls and immediately adopted by all others. No matter how overused (even by a candidate, who represented nothing more than a continuation of what we have seen for almost eight years), it still reflects what America is longing for. No more pampering the rich few and the powerful big corporations, no more wars, no more ignoring today's needy and future generations, no more pilfering of this country's resources and neglecting its maintenance, no more downplaying the man-made problems our planet is faced with, no more arrogance towards America's friends and allies – the list goes on and on, and the urgent need to repair the damage caused by disastrous mismanagement is obvious to many.

I look at the situation from the lowly perspective of a resident, who came to this country more than 35 years ago in spite of the grave problems then: the Vietnamese War, lacking civil rights for many of its citizens, and belligerent Cold War foreign policy. Meeting average Americans and representatives of its intellectual elite made us stay beyond the planned two years – a country that great with people that committed and resources that abundant simply had to get better. The gamble paid off; The Vietnamese war was ended, civil rights were signed into law for all (I know, not perfect yet, but what a progress), and the Cold War was won. The United States prospered under various Democratic and Republican presidents, and we were ready to finally apply for citizenship in the country that might well have been the best of all, when disaster struck and most of the progress achieved over decades was abolished in less than eight years.

Now America is back by actually more than thirty years: In the middle of another terrible war that should never have been started, with civil rights trampled even below the Geneva Convention, and a Cold War scenario rising again on the horizon. What a difference one president, his gang of four and the extreme elements in the population he arose can make. From being the star of the free world, America has fallen to be an ideological bully trampling on much people hold dear worldwide.

So now we have to hope for change again, even more so than in the seventies. Yes, America can end the Iraq war, re-affirm the commitment to human rights, avoid another Cold War and befriend its old allies again, who would like nothing more. Short of a revolution, that could only happen through the democratic process we trust: Dump as many of the bums in Congress as possible, America, and elect a president, who can lead you back to where this country belongs. If true change is what is needed (and I wholeheartedly agree), the choice between a veteran senator (who strongly supported Bush in his 2004 reelection campaign, voted with him 90% of the time and promised to continue his disastrous economic and foreign policies) and a dynamic newcomer was an easy one for many.

May the next president now be able to fill the hollow platitudes of hope and change with real action, with the support of a better than do-nothing Congress. Then America will shine again as the beacon of the free world, and I would be delighted finally to apply for citizenship and honored, if granted.

CHRISTMAS SPIRIT

One of the few memories I have of my childhood is that of Christmas Eve. After a traditional, very modest dinner an angel would ring the glass bell, the door would open, and there was the Christmas tree in all its splendor – a real fir, with real candles flickering. We would sing "*Stille Nacht*" and "*Ihr Kinderlein kommet*", and eventually get around to opening the packages under the tree – exciting for me as a child, but even then not the most important part of the evening

When we were adults living in the foothills of the Bavarian Alps, the presents became of course even less relevant, but the festive spirit was still there. Whether at home or on a skiing vacation in a tiny village in the Swiss Alps – there was snow, a dark sky sparkling with myriads of stars, and the knowledge that something very special had happened two thousand years ago.

Now fast-forward to Xmas American-style. "White Christmas" and "Jingle Bells" accompany you in supermarkets and department stores after Thanksgiving at the latest, and – believe it or not – we had to listen to it as early as August in a never to be revisited shop in Pennsylvania. By the time you pull your plastic tree out of the closet and plug in the electric candles, you have had enough and just rush through buying last minute presents, the bigger the better.

Do I ever get homesick? Rarely, since we love this country with all its little flaws and deficiencies. Christmas, however, is one of the times.

CHURCH AND STATE

One of the most frequently emphasized components of democracy in America is the strict separation of church and state, while in less democratic countries such as Germany Christians are even forced to support their church through taxes collected by the federal government. How then is this fundamental difference reflected in people's everyday life?

American school children pledge daily allegiance to "one nation under God" and receive their allowance in legal tender proclaiming, "In God we trust" (Which may be a good idea, considering the federal budget deficit). I know of no other civilized country identifying itself that closely with religion, with the possible exception of certain fundamentalist Islamic ones that most Americans would probably rather not be compared to. No American candidate for public office would ever dare to admit to being less than a devote believer in one of the generally accepted variations of Christianity, or immediately loose any chance to be elected. Instead, it behooves him/her to be seen on TV attending Sunday mass, preferably of course in a predominantly African-American or Hispanic congregation, or at least in a small rural community (You might as well kill a couple of birds with one stone). And every politician simply has to end any speech by invoking God's blessing; some even claim to have God as a personal advisor.

In contrast, the constituents in France, Germany, Italy, etc. seemingly could not care less about the religious orientation of their leaders. Religion is considered a private matter of no relevance to the job performance of politicians. And if you don't want to pay *Kirchensteuer* (church tax) in Germany, you formally declare your separation from the church, and are off the hook. Which by the way will not keep you from being able to attend mass and even receive communion. So explain to me again that separation of church and state – where it is preached and where practiced.

At the popular basis, things look a bit clearer. Fervent believers in democracy initiate lawsuits (a favorite American pastime) to have a small bible monument removed from a public building; in San Diego, a decade-long legal struggle is still going on about the cross on top of Mt. Soledad, a local landmark and in my opinion much less offensive than the microwave towers adorning most other mountain tops in the area. As a European, I am used to hiking in the Alps, where every self-respecting summit is crowned by a *Gipfelkreuz* (summit cross). Seeing that has no religious significance to me, but simply means that I finally made it to the top and can rest under this marker, which is often quite beautiful and reflects local craftsmanship. (But then I am an agnostic and don't object to symbols of religion or their propagators, as long as the latter don't proselytize. You guessed that already, right?)

Does that indicate, I wonder, that Europeans are just apathetic – or, heaven (!) forbid, perhaps more tolerant than Americans? Isn't tolerance yet another cornerstone of American democracy? I ponder this issue watching a tele-evangelist and his mesmerized audience, and the news with pictures of faces and posters of pro-life demonstrators. I turn off the TV when I hear about the murder of a doctor who has performed abortions, since I know these are just isolated exceptions in this country of tolerance, with strict separation of church and state. God bless America.

CITIZENSHIP

After 30 years of a good life in this country, we still cannot make up our mind to become naturalized – what is wrong with us? Let me try to explain.

When we first arrived here in 1972, just married and with fresh advanced degrees, it was with a great deal of apprehension. The Vietnam war, the black struggle for civil rights, and many other issues were on our young and idealistic minds, and my main reason for coming was the opportunity of a couple of postdoctoral years at Harvard, combined with vacations to experience some of the great natural wonders we had seen so many pictures of.

Within a few months, everything changed. Struggling to make a living with little money and virtually no personal belongings in the overwhelmingly confusing big city of Boston, we were immediately helped by our landlady and her friends, all Jewish and not necessarily expected to embrace young Germans of all people. They did, however, and in little time we started to feel at home and to consider changing allegiance.

Decades later we still haven't, after a fairly successful career living comfortably in southern California (arguably one of the most pleasant parts of the world), with a son born American, married to an All-American wife and enjoying their life with their son, dog, house and cars as all Americans should be able to. Instead we are holding on to our Green Cards (by now pink) and are reluctant to apply for citizenship in this great nation.

Is it because of George W. Bush, the best the citizens of this country could find and reelect as leader of the free world? Is it because of an educational system that leaves the average American less cultivated and sophisticated than most elementary school graduates in any European country? Is it because we don't want to carry the same passport as people who believe in the bible verbatim and refuse to accept revolutionary theories such as evolution as a reflection of the Almighty's grand plan? Is it because we don't want to be seen by the rest of the world as members of a violent and trigger-happy bunch, who readily accepts thousands of gun shot victims every year as a small price to pay for the right to enrich everybody's life through the possession of firearms?

Initially I thought these perceived flaws were simply the dark side of tolerance in a society which accommodates flaming liberals as well as macho rednecks, passionate pro-lifers as well as pro choice-advocates, tree huggers and Hummer owners. Until I realized that true tolerance means accepting individuals different from the mainstream, even if the latter is as broad as it is here. America has always accommodated different cultures and ethnic backgrounds, but is it really the melting pot of lore?

Environmentally oriented and spending our spare time hiking and birdwatching, back in the seventies we were sneered upon as "old ladies in tennis shoes"; now of course we would be "in", if we cared to be. Oh no, I forgot – we smoke, and that makes us outcasts again, at par with pedophiles and other perverts (Actually, pedophiles aren't all that bad). So we smoke our cigarettes at a small section of airport curb set aside for us deviates, and longingly watch the healthy non-smoking crowd happily inhaling the exhaust fumes of cabs and shuttle buses, waiting with running engines to support their environmentally friendly air conditionings.

Of course I should not be griping about the missionary fervor of fellow human beings, who simply know what would be best for me. (*"Am deutschen Wesen soll die Welt genesen"* is what inspired many Germans during World War I – The German Way of Life will make the world a better place. Sounds familiar?) A little harassment every now and then is no big deal, and anti-smoking, anti-abortion and anti-anything are only beneficial, as was prohibition (for the Mafia). As long as gays are only occasionally beaten to death and African-Americans are not routinely dragged behind pick-ups, tolerance must be alive and well.

So for the umpteenth time: Why have we not yet tried to become citizens? If we don't yet love America enough, should we leave it, as some compassionate conservatives would undoubtedly recommend? Definitely not, as long as we still have hope that this society will grow up, that one day problem-solving will not include the use of a hand gun, that not all fossils will have to be 5,000 years old to fit into one creationist week, that women can decide whether they want their baby or not without having to worry about their doctor's life, and that you don't have to shoot up beer cans in the desert or mountain-bike in Lycra pants to be accepted as a real outdoors person. This country has already come a long way despite recent set-backs, and the dream of a truly tolerant society is no longer far-fetched (neither here nor in Germany). Individuals with lawful interests and preferences somewhat different from their neighbors' or community standards will be gladly accommodated, and the rest of the world will no longer have to worry about being bombed into adopting the American way of life.

Then the choice will be easy, and we will gladly trade our red passports against blue ones, which will then be just as welcome anywhere in the world. Americans will no longer be judged by the size of their home and the material of their counter tops, the make and year of their car and the price of their watch, but will have an internal yard stick by which to measure happiness, success and yes, morale. They will live up to and apologize for their sins of the past from the expulsion of Native Americans to slavery to the encampment of Japanese-Americans during World War II, they will no longer allow the repeat of what happened to Passenger Pigeons and Carolina Parakeets, and Jenny Jones and Gerry Springer will no longer have a fan club. Immigrants would no longer flock to the US just for economic reasons. The nouveau-rich Wall Street whiz won't be there to complain about the sad state of affairs, which threatens to force him to work beyond the age of 31, and driving back in our 10 year-old car from a desert hike we will no longer have to endure the sight of discarded sofas and bullet-ridden refrigerators.

Then we will know that Americans will have learnt to truly appreciate the fantastic wealth and unrivaled beauty of their country, and to coexist in harmony with each other and their environment. If we live long enough to experience that, I would be so honored and proud to fly the Star - Spangled Banner wherever I go.

If I ever had reason to hope to see this dream come true, it is now, after the recent presidential election. Of course I am happy for the African-American minority that a half-black person was chosen to be the next president, but I am even happier for the white majority, many of whom have managed to overcome atavistic racial bias to select the most qualified candidate with no regard for his skin color. That many of these voters were young people makes me even more optimistic about this country's future.

CLIMATE CHANGE

As everybody who has ever heard about ice ages knows, our planet's climate has always oscillated between hot and cold periods during the 13.7 billion years of its existence. Also no news is the observation that we are presently in an accelerated warming cycle; in fact for more than two decades scientists from various disciplines have tried to alert us (Remember those warnings about greenhouse gases or the hole in the ozone layer?), and the 1979 oil crisis sent an unmistakable message. New is only that the symptoms can no longer be ignored even by those completely unaware of or actively opposed to any scientific progress, including the 43rd president of these United States (to whom, however, the $ 1.8 Million campaign contributions by oil companies in 2000 seem to have sent an even clearer message).

The only legitimate topics of discussion can be, How bad is the situation, How much have we humans contributed to it, and What can we do to improve it? While the first two questions are certainly also important, the one that really matters is the last – since no matter how severe the problem is and who is to blame, it is in our utmost survival interest to stop or at least slow down the warming trend. Here as in many other life-or-death situations, the old American adage "Don't fix what is not broken" must not be applied. As any engineer will confirm, many stress points are easier and less costly to relieve before an accident occurs, and in some cases the damage resulting from procrastination can actually be beyond repair (The world's climate would be one).

Engineers are also among those who can help alleviate the problem. Many have already found out that a gallon of gasoline can take a vehicle a lot farther than 12 or 20 miles, and some have discovered that Msrs. Otto and Diesel have not invented the only means to propel an automobile. From modest steps like replacing 60 single passenger cars with a natural gas-powered bus and repairable or recyclable instead of disposable consumer goods, to more fundamental changes such as the greater use of oil and coal independent energy sources (hydro, geothermal, wind, solar, tidal, wave and yes, as an interim solution, the dreaded but quite safe nuclear) there are already numerous alternatives to our present reckless pilfering of earth's resources; others could be discovered with the support of visionary governments not solely committed to helping corporations meet their short-term profit targets. "Old" Europe has started to blaze the trail; when will the New World with its larger resources and its (past?) ingenuity follow? Drilling for more oil off the California coast and in the Arctic National Wildlife Refuge are not the answer, nor the destruction of Canada's boreal forest for the surface mining of tar sands. If impoverished villages in Ethiopia and in the Argentinean Andes can cook, heat and light their huts with solar energy (often installed with the help of micro-loans and European engineers volunteering their time), and if Spain manages to run large-scale photovoltaic power plants, shouldn't the world's biggest economy be able to wean itself from its addiction to fossil fuels? At least, when it will no longer be dominated by oil companies, their lobbyists and their paid alumni, one would hope.

Will serious efforts on humanity's side guarantee the iconic polar bear's survival in the wild? Possibly not, but they would greatly increase the chances for many more generations of humans to enjoy a decent life on this, our only, earth. (Contrary to some futuristic but unrealistic suggestions, mankind is not a "two planet species", and Mars is neither within reach nor an attractive alternative to our blue planet.)

If on the other hand we don't change our destructive habits or – just as well – spend much more time investigating, discussing and administering the problem rather than addressing it (Analysis can turn into paralysis, the doers and shakers used to say in the old days), then we won't have to worry about the finite lifetime of our sun or asteroids, super-volcanoes and other natural catastrophes: We'll be enough of a disaster to make this planet uninhabitable for mankind without any help. Keep in mind that presently about 6 billion members of our species populate a world, the carrying capacity of which is estimated to be 4 billion – and 8 billion are already in the forecast. While we are the most dangerous super-predator ever to evolve and at the top of every food chain, we should also have the brain to be wise (not just street-smart) and voluntarily limit our capability to overexploit our environment. If not, our race is bound sooner rather than later to follow the way of the Mayas, Anasazis, Mississippians and others who completely exhausted their resources. (That was probably not the only reason for their demise. Too many wars and religious fanaticism also contributed, not a comforting thought considering our present situation.)

All that does not seem to be a very important issue. Although everybody pretends to care so much about future generations, during the past campaign only 0.02% of the questions posed to presidential candidates by voters related to Global Warming. Hopefully this does not mean that we will become nothing more than another evolutionary dead end and force Mother Nature to try a different approach.

Collar Color

In everyday life, the imaginary color of your equally imaginary collar categorizes you unequivocally. Is it blue, you are probably not very highly educated, work hard for your and your family's living, and don't have much sense (nor time and money) for relishing the subtle pleasures of life. Is it white, your advanced degree gives you more responsibility in your profession, you leave the hard labor to others, and your refined taste allows you to savor mankind's cultural achievements. Now that we have clarified this distinction, I am wondering about what color my own collar might be.

As a university student (clearly white), I worked during the academic summer vacation in junk yards dragging huge chunks of rusty iron around, or in a car wash, until my hands were shriveled like prunes (It doesn't get much bluer). During the semester, one of my tasks as a teaching assistant (white) was to collect intestinal parasites while wading through ankle-deep pig excrements in a slaughterhouse (Any doubts about the color?).

Even during my thesis work, my collar color was decidedly mixed. There was advanced laboratory work with sophisticated instruments alternating with studies in the library – but spending 14 hours without break in a walk-in freezer to finally be rewarded with a curry sausage late at night at a fast food stand did not strike me as particularly white.

My subsequent professional career then did give me ample opportunity to sample true white collar work. I did meet high-flying Wall street types and executives raking in huge rewards (sometimes for putting blue-collar employees out of work), but I also took occasional breaks trying to fix our ancient car or cleaning up after a tornado in the countryside – so fairly white with a few blue specks.

Now that the Golden Years of retirement have arrived, however, I find myself back to almost all blue. Between house repairs and serious yard work (pruning trees, digging new irrigation lines, weeding and watering) there is barely enough time to read and write, circumstances I share with a good friend and fellow scientist. While we joke about having gotten our advanced degrees for these activities, I am convinced that it is really good for us. Not only does it save money twice (we need to neither hire gardeners nor pay for gym memberships, as our truly white-collared neighbors do), but we are also constantly reminded that it is old-fashioned physical labor our fine-feathered friends' lifestyle is based on.

CONSERVATION

The need to conserve resources and protect the environment has finally made it into the mainstream. It is no longer an idea pushed solely by day-dreaming do-gooders, but even the most reckless developers find themselves forced by reality and public opinion to accept limitations on unbridled growth at any price.

On the other hand, environmentalists will have to compromise, too. While they may find it hard to swallow, we will not be able to shelter every species against humankind's activities and needs. From a biodiversity point of view, some losses will be less grave than others – an important point to consider when setting priorities. There are for example about 50 different species of Blues (tiny to small butterflies) in North America alone, and while the extinction of any of these often very local species would be regrettable and should be avoided, its disappearance would not be as much of a blow as for instance the loss of the platypus or any other organism with no or few similar relatives. Which, by the way, does not suggest that sacrificing the Redondo Blue for yet another strip mall or an additional freeway lane would be justified…

Whenever decisions directly affecting the well-being or even survival of a rare plant or animal are being made, it must be kept in mind that the presence of an endangered or threatened species more often than not also indicates that the survival of an unusual and precious whole habitat may be at stake, with all its other inhabitants.

CREDIT

One of the first revelations after coming to America is the importance of a high credit score. As a foreigner without any credit history documented by the three major repositories of this essential information, you are almost non-existent and certainly not worthy of any organization's trust. To gain that, you better start borrowing money as soon as possible and buy as many preferably expensive things as you can physically accommodate. The latter is difficult only in the beginning, when you are issued a credit card with a spending limit of $500, but don't despair. If you faithfully make your minimum monthly payment, your credit line will soon start to rise to dizzying heights, allowing you to run up a $40,000 debt on one card (Between my wife and me, we carry three, one actually without any spending limit at all). Add to this a couple of cars (financed, of course), furniture (no payment for the next three years) and the jumbo mortgage for your palatial abode, and you are well on your way to become a highly desirable and trustworthy customer vied for by any financial institution and department store, as proven by the incessant flood of pre-approved new credit card applications in your daily mail.

To accomplish this goal (the true American dream?), you will of course have to work hard and may need your partner's income, too. That then will enable you to afford a nanny, gardener, lawn and pool service, dog-walker, maid and shopping services – all of which you will need to compensate for your long hours on the job(s). You will even be in a position to dine out frequently (good, since neither of you has the time to cook) or at least grab some fast food on your way home, and to afford expensive health insurance, which will come handy considering your "active lifestyle".

That is about the time for the latest revelation, summarized in buzz-words like sub-prime mortgages, credit crunch and stagflation. You start to understand your old-fashioned mother's (or was it your grandmother's?) "What goes up, must come down", and why your ridiculously risk-averse dad kept mumbling about a house of cards. And having marveled about pawn-shops and the viability of the paycheck-advance industry (Who would not have enough savings to cover an unexpected car repair?), I am finally getting it: Even with an ample supply of sleeping pills generously provided by the government and large corporations, no dream lasts forever, and the awakening can be awfully rude.

(This was written about a year ago. Since then, the wake-up call has occurred, and loud enough to be heard around the world.)

CULTS

No other civilized country seems to be home to as many cults as the United States. It does not matter what off-the-wall gospel any crackpot comes up with – he will attract a group of followers, who firmly believe and live by what he preaches.

Polygamy? Of course. Impregnating a 12 year-old girl? That's what she was created for. Aliens bringing the truth to earthlings, golden tablets presented by God to a traveling salesman, no problem. The whole universe created some 5,000 years ago? Why not. Letting your child starve to death? If it's God's will. Whether you speak in tongues, expect the world to come to an end in 2012 or rely on rattlesnakes to identify the true believers, you will find a congregation happy to welcome you.

Citizens of most other developed countries are satisfied with the selection offered by the established major religions; why are many Americans not? Is it because they are so independent-minded that they need home-brews in addition? Or are they so disillusioned by a materialistic and superficial society that they need stronger moral support and a more idealistic alternative than offered by traditional religions, which are often themselves tainted or corrupted?

Whatever the underlying reasons, the advantages are clear. If my health problem cannot be resolved by a doctor, I won't need to travel to the South American rainforest to see a shaman – the local faith healer will do; any psychic can help me track him down. And if it works, I should be able to find a televangelist to take credit for it and spread the good news, Praise the Lord.

Curb Appeal

Although this is a term a new resident should learn and understand quickly, "Curb Appeal" is not a word easily looked up in a dictionary. It relates to the frontal view of a house, which is supposed to reflect at least its owners' sense of neatness and beauty, preferably also their wealth and important standing in the community. Manicured flowerbeds, an immaculate lawn and a well-maintained driveway are essential; an impressive covered main entrance (maybe flanked by columns of any style) helps significantly. Fake windows and doors leading nowhere, and even walls similar to the props of a western movie adorn shopping centers in southern California. The backyard, on the other hand, is quite irrelevant, as no casual (but oh so important) passer-by is likely ever to see it – so anything from a personal junkyard to a toxic waste dump will do.

This emphasis on superficial appearance is but one reflection of the overall philosophy of valuing style over substance – exactly the opposite of the old (outdated?) guideline many Europeans were raised to follow: "*Mehr sein als scheinen*" (Be more than you seem). Keeping up with the Jones, name dropping and bragging are all indicators of the same sad lack of an internal value system and its replacement with the need for acclaim by just about anybody.

Is this a general weakness of modern human beings or peculiar to the American society? Travel to Mexico's mountain town of

Cuernavaca, where you can tell the residences of American retirees at a glance ("Because they let it all hang out", comment of a local), or to Camogli on the Italian Riviera, where some modest townhouses by the harbor can only be identified as remodeled by the rich because of the presence of an inconspicuous intercom next to the door (But wait until you step inside!). Of course you can make similar surprise discoveries at German farm houses or fisher cottages, or in France or in Greece. And as you travel, do you ever notice that the bigger a Mercedes or BMW is on the road in Germany, the more likely it is not to have any model-identifier on its trunk lid, while here you proudly advertise your car's characteristics (if available, in gold rather than chrome letters)? If you cannot afford that, then at least a bumper sticker might brag that you are the proud parent of the high school student of the month.

In some American corporations, boasting is actually mandatory. In a former job, I had to fight with the CEO to be allowed the same office furniture as my direct reports (I find mahogany depressing) and to drive only a mid-size company car. At least I did not have to put up plaques on my office wall reflecting past exams and awards.

Maybe the continuous display of one's real or perceived accomplishments and the accompanying admiration by others provides great daily satisfaction – but the occasional comment of a flabbergasted visitor to our home ("I would never have guessed that you have such a paradise behind your house!") makes us smile instead. And I still relish the memory of a reception at the German embassy in Washington, when the Cultural Attaché turned from me in contempt after I told him I was the homemaker to my wife, the invited teacher at the German school in Potomac. Admittedly I had even more fun, when a few weeks later the same person called the National Cancer Institute to ask for a Molecular Biologist to evaluate a sensational (but in the end fake) new cancer treatment by German scientists, and ended up with the homemaker. So

"*Mehr sein als scheinen*" still has its rewards – plus you don't have to worry about adjustable mortgages for a house you should never have bought. Somehow ignoring old-fashioned attitudes has a way of catching up with people.

Customer Service

I am not talking about the "How are you?" or "Have a nice day" at the supermarket check-out (Although it makes you feel good, they could not care less how you are, or whether the rest of your day will be nice or rotten), but about when you actually need service. Try to exchange an item you mistakenly bought in Germany (wrong size, color, etc.) but that is not defective, versus having the same problem here, and you will notice a glaring difference.

Here I have returned without receipt hiking boots that fell apart after a year, or plumbing parts since I did not measure correctly – good luck with that in the Old Country. In the US, items you buy as a present often come with a gift receipt that does not reveal the purchase price, but allows easy exchange. The old adage "The customer is always right" usually holds true here but rarely there, so enjoy it while it lasts (Lately things have started to change due to, what else, abuse by the beneficiaries of this attitude).

Telephone Customer Service by the "Customer Relations Specialists" or "Service Associates" (many other titles are invented daily) of big companies are a different story, however. If you are lucky enough to talk to a representative whose English you can understand despite his/her thick Indian accent, you may not get anywhere, unless you manage to be connected with or get called back by a supervisor. Even then, only your hint about complaining to a state or federal regulatory agency might give results. Not that said supervisor actually wants to help you obtain what is rightfully yours – but the overhead-heavy paperwork the authorities would require often makes a reluctant company give in to your demands.

So don't be deterred by the fact that telephone reps only have first names like Larry or Bob (their accent not withstanding), but be persistent. In Germany, by the way, people have last names, although that does not mean you will get anywhere with them soon either. If you have serious problems, you are better off here, since there is a general prejudice favoring the little guy (you and me) over big recalcitrant organizations. It does take time and effort sometimes, but if you are the Michael Kohlhaas-type (I am, and I won't let them get away wit it), you have a good chance of prevailing in the end, especially if you are fortunate enough to have the support of an organization with high visibility. Local or (even better) national media coverage of your struggle is unsurpassed, but I once succeeded in forcing my health insurance to pay an ambulance bill with only the unwavering help of a dedicated accountant in our Fire Department. It took a year and a half though; needless to say, I have since changed my insurance.

That is one of the advantages of our free market economy. If you feel abused by a corporation or just get unsatisfactory service, be it an insurance, bank or ISP, their competitors are always happy to welcome you as a new customer.

DARK AGES

Every country and every continent have had their Dark Ages, periods in their history they would rather forget, but should not. Best known in Europe are probably those medieval times of famine, wars of unspeakable cruelty, and exploitation of the poor by the ruthless nobility. In spite of that widespread suffering, several countries added on more dark periods – Spain the inquisition and in fairly recent history, the tens of thousands of Disappeared under Franco's dictatorship; Germany the Third Reich with the horror of the holocaust; the Balkans the ethnic cleansing and mass murder after the disintegration of Yugoslavia; Turkey the annihilation of a large part of the Armenian population.

The Americas have had their Dark Ages, too – not just the one brought by the conquistadores and missionaries upon the Aztecs, but also homemade ones. From the Mayas and their human sacrifices to Pinochet (with even more people disappearing than in fascist Spain) to Brazil's reckless extermination of rain forest tribes in the way of progress, many South American countries have ignominious chapters in their history. North America fared no better – from the anachronism of slavery to the brutal expulsion of the natives despite scores of treaties never kept to the internment of Japanese-Americans during World War II. In Australia, by the way, the Aborigines were not much better off under their European invaders.

Africa is going through Dark Ages now, with genocide being commonplace from Ruanda to Darfur to Nigeria. Millions of innocent people have been and still are being raped, mutilated and slaughtered, while the industrialized (and more civilized?) world is voicing serious disapproval, but not much more. And even Asia, home to some of the oldest cultures on earth, will in the future probably not look back with pride on fanatic fundamentalism, terrorism or the Chinese version of human rights, not to forget the slaughter of millions of Cambodians by the Khmer Rouge.

Do countries learn from their Dark Age experience? Certainly not from that of others, as just like human individuals they only seem to be able to learn from their own mistakes – otherwise history would not have to repeat itself all over the world. The domestic lessons have worked, however. Germany after having started and lost two world wars is now probably one of the most pacifist countries in the world (much to the chagrin of the US, who would love to see the *Bundeswehr* fight in Afghanistan and Iraq). The same is true for Japan – after having experienced the horror of nuclear war in their home country, even the friendly visit by an American nuclear warship triggers massive demonstrations. South America is trying to come to grips with its history by prosecuting the culprits of the past, as are part of the Balkans and South Africa. And the US? While the Dark Ages are not easily remembered (Just ask your teenage child, how much they learn in school about those...), democracy and human rights are by now so engrained in its population that the country seems safe, if one is willing to ignore temporary relapses like Guantanamo.

If now Europe, Australia and North America would only help the rest of the world to move out of its Dark Ages into a bright future.

DEATH

Everybody knows that death is an intrinsic part of life, can happen anytime (Beware of the mail truck) and at some point with certainty will. So it would behoove you and me to accept its unavoidability and be ready for it, whether it hits you or one of your loved ones.

And yet many people prefer to live in continuous denial, avoid the topic in conversations and in their thoughts, and do whatever they can to postpone the inevitable. Even aging is a process to be avoided or at least hidden, to the great benefit of the chemical industry and cosmetic surgeons.

I find this trend most amazing with self-professed religious believers, who should actually be looking forward to a happy and eternal afterlife. Instead many of them are just as afraid of dying as atheists, who have a more understandable problem coping with existentialism.

As an agnostic, I am simply curious to find out who is right, although I am not in any particular rush. Of one thing I am already certain: neither I nor anybody else will disappear without trace. Once you are buried, your disintegrating body's molecules will eventually be incorporated in other living things, a fact many "primitive" cultures reflect in their belief that the spirits of their ancestors live in plants and animals. Even if you are cremated, nothing gets lost but continues as fertile ashes and free energy (thus unfortunately adding to global warming).

Just as your body continues in bits and pieces, so does your mind in the memories of your friends and relatives and in any lasting contributions you may have made to some aspect of human culture. And if you have ever had a strong déjà-vue experience, you are possibly inclined to carry the survival of the mind even a step further.

DEMOCRACY

There is no doubt in my mind that democracy is the best form of government humans have developed so far. It works truly well, however, only in a population of well-educated independent thinkers, who can choose deliberately from a selection of the most qualified for public office. The head of government should then be supported but also be controlled by a legislative branch, to provide continuous checks and balances – as nobody must be above the law. So goes the theory; reality unfortunately varies from country to country. From time to time, even the world's most democratic one (where the candidates for the highest office are elected in primaries, not selected by a group of peers) can end up with a head of state not representing the majority of its citizens, as demonstrated by subsequent abysmal approval ratings. Not to forget the Palestinians, who in democratic elections voted for Hamas and are now paying the price.

Does anybody, Democrat, Republican or Independent believe these days that the candidates running for the highest office in this country were always the cream of the crop the nation has produced? Are the voters generally well-educated careful thinkers as in a meritocracy, or do at least all the well-educated vote? Watching the many debates and hearing or reading excerpts from campaign speeches and other statements, one could hardly avoid coming to a different conclusion.

To be a viable candidate today, it helps to be independently wealthy – in itself not necessarily a sign of quality. In fact, some of the wealthier people in the country have never done anything positive to deserve their riches, but either inherited them or used more than doubtful means to get there. Are these role models, and does that qualify them to lead the beacon of democracy, which the US should be, through the next four to eight years? Secondly, in any competition between similarly qualified contenders, often the most reckless one will win. Whether as CEO, Prime Minister or President, you should be willing to walk over corpses ("*über Leichen gehen*", is the German idiom) to come in first. Keep that in mind during you decision-making process – most of the contenders are not "nice people". And finally, any successful candidate tries to show utmost flexibility when talking to different audiences. He or she has to be pro-life and pro-choice, pro-family values and homophile, for ending the Iraq war and for winning it at any cost, for universal healthcare and guaranteed social security without tax increases, for a free market without big government intervention but protection for the poor sub-prime mortgage holders and their lenders, for strong border protection but liberal immigration policies, for separation of church and state in one nation under god, for protecting the environment without impeding industrial growth and inconveniencing big corporations, for respecting human rights and civil liberties while being tough as nails on terrorists, and, and, and. Impossible? Not at all – just look at who is vying for your vote, they all can do it, one more oblivious of past statements to the contrary than the other. Would you buy a used car from any of them? Then vote for him or her!

With doubtful candidates, do at least the voters pass the litmus test? In the past, only about half of who is entitled to cast a ballot actually did, and the demographics were pretty scary. Many of the best-educated did not bother to vote, but those who did were not necessarily the ones whose judgment you would trust.

Whether motivated by religious fervor, fear of imaginary or real terrorist attacks, or literally driven to the polling stations – will their choice be rational and give this nation the most competent and unifying president it so urgently needs, after years under the least qualified and most divisive in recent history? Or are we down to the "100 billion flies can't be wrong – poop must taste good"-type democracy?

Now how about the overseeing legislative, from which many of the presidential candidates are recruited? Is this Congress doing its job of representing the people, counterbalancing an out-of-control president, pursuing the best interest of the country? You be the judge, but it has not earned the pet name "Do Nothing Congress" without reason. Yes, it does represent people's interests, as long as these are limited to their local constituencies (That's why the pork barrel is full of earmarks), but the nation's? Thousands of full-time lobbyists waving money and influence make sure that doesn't happen, unless it also benefits their employers. Any new member of Congress, House or Senate, will need to learn the rules of this game really fast, if they want to last longer than one term (and the vast majority are really long-term, which tells you something).

So does democracy suck? No, definitely not – it is the best of all necessarily imperfect solutions humankind has come up with. But in this best of all countries (She really can and should be that), it has been seriously compromised by indifference of the majority, demagoguery of its ideological leaders, and power hunger and greed of the people's representatives. Can it be fixed? Of course, but it will take an effort. First, "Throw out the bums", get rid of as many members as possible of the "Old Boys Club" (which includes a few girls), and replace them with newcomers committed to change, no matter of which party affiliation. Trust me – a new Democrat will work harder than an established Republican, and a new Republican will be better for the country than an oh so comfortable Democrat. Then select the one presidential candidate from the admittedly not overly impressive pool, whom you think you can trust to be best for this country (Remember the used car rule!), and keep you fingers crossed. And most important of all: DO VOTE, whatever your choice may be. This is one of the most important privileges (and also duties) in a working democracy, and "I did not vote for him/her" is not going to be a valid excuse, if you did not vote at all.

(This was written a while ago, in the middle of frequently rather ugly primaries. While many of the general remarks still hold true, this election has alleviated some of my greatest fears. Voter participation was at an all-time high, including many young people frequently suspected of indifference, and the candidate who won does not seem to be the most ruthless but rather the most caring. Congratulations, America! Now let's hope that with your ongoing support the future president will be able to live up to your expectations.)

Deregulation

Rules and regulations are just as necessary as laws to keep a society living and working in harmony. The universal problem that they like bureaucracies often tend to take on a life of their own (think OSHA) of course needs to be watched and controlled as much as possible.

If instead you truly think that smart people, who have decided that the only thing that matters in life is the accumulation of vast amounts of money for themselves and the organization they work for, can and will police themselves, you have to be a strong believer in Republican fairytales. The result to be expected should now be obvious even to the story-tellers.

Fortunately the risk is quite limited to companies, if they are only big enough. You can rest assured that the government will not allow them to go belly-up, but that they will be bailed out with the money those dumb and risk-averse taxpayers have faithfully paid in (and then some, which however can luckily be passed on with all the other accumulated debt to future generations of happy Americans).

Only the executives responsible for the mess will have to pay heavily for their unbridled greed. As punishment, they will possibly receive only a paltry $60 million bonus for bankrupting their institution, instead of the customary $150 million plus. Maybe the government should also create a hardship fund to help these victims through their suffering.

DIET

Humans are, for all we can tell from our anatomy and metabolism, omnivorous. We don't have the specialized enzyme equipment of a Koala (Eucalyptus leaves only) or a Giant Panda (Bamboo please) or the teeth of predators, nor the multiple stomachs of vegan ruminants, but are in the same category as bears and – sorry – pigs. We certainly need our fruit and vegetables (Obligatory meat eaters like tigers or other cats don't get scurvy), but if we had evolved to be vegetarians, our pearly whites would look more like those of a deer or a bison.

Which points to what your parents hopefully already told you: a balanced diet. This does not mean fast food plus supplements from your supermarket or health store shelves, but a mix of animal protein and greens similar to what former generations consumed, if they could afford it. As we know, even the best supplements cannot replace the natural mix of vitamins, minerals, cofactors and trace elements in Mother Nature's vegetables and meats – actually, out-of-balance goodies could be bad for you (Ever heard of hypervitaminoses?). Even the health fad of the day, antioxidants, could be too much of a good thing. While they catch cancer-causing free radicals, some of those aggressive oxygen molecules are needed to start certain slow but important reactions in a healthy metabolism.

In general, supplements other than your daily multivitamin or calcium should be used very judiciously, if at all. While many of them provide at best a placebo effect and are known to be truly beneficial only to their manufacturer (just like those hugely overpriced juices from Siberian miracle plants), some actually contain powerful active ingredients in mostly not standardized amounts and can be dangerous, especially when taken in addition to serious prescription drugs. St. John's Wort is probably the best known in this category, but not the only one.

So the old truism applies to diet as to almost everything else: Don't go to extremes, but keep to the middle ground. And if you long for an *occasional* hamburger with those terribly unhealthy fries, just give in – especially now, when even the gurus have found out that being *a little* "overweight" is actually good for you. Watch out for the *little*, though – more than a third of American children ages 6 to 19 are *seriously* overweight, half of them what is called obese. More than two thirds of them may end up as overweight adults, with all the accompanying health and emotional problem.

DRESSING CASUAL

Americans have always been known for dressing casually rather than formally in everyday life, and even many companies observe "casual Friday", unless you are dealing with customers or important business partners.

Lately, however, this attitude has been carried to an extreme that is not just bad taste, but makes people look like slobs. This is not limited to teenagers wearing oversized skating pants revealing their underwear and – especially chic – part of their buttocks, but includes their role models on stage. Of course rock stars don't necessarily have to dress up like Elvis or Fred Astaire, but does that really have to mean tank tops and torn jeans like a construction worker on the job?

Dressing down does not stop at the youngest generation. Even in concerts or at the opera, much of the audience shows up in blue jeans (or shorts; this is Southern California) and flannel shirts or Ts, not even in country club-casual slacks and polo shirts. So much for the festive atmosphere... A pleasant break is usually provided by Latinos and Asian-Americans, whose culture (not only in this respect) seems more similar to that of Europe – a part of the proverbial "Old World Charm" that would be easy to emulate, if one cared.

DRINKING AGE

There probably was a legal drinking age in Germany when I grew up – I just did not know about it. When as a teenager I went to a restaurant with my parents, I had a beer with lunch or dinner as part of the ritual, but did not particularly care for its bitter taste (As opposed to most American beers, German Pils does have a flavor). At special events at home (birthdays, Christmas and the likes) I joint my parents for a glass of wine or champagne and never felt the urge for more, although it would probably have been ok.

After I moved to the closest university town and was on my own at the tender age of 18, my favorite drinks were milk and during long nights of cramming several cups of espresso; my alcohol consumption was usually limited to an occasional small glass of Port or Tokay wine. There was simply no incentive for binge drinking, since I knew alcohol and did not have to prove to myself or anybody else that I was now an adult and entitled to lots of it.

Several times I ended up in company enticing me to drink hard liquor, sometimes too much of it, and the resulting bad hang-over made me avoid it for decades to come. Even now I rarely have a brandy (mostly after a heavy dinner, if at all) or a cocktail (preferably a long drink on a hot summer day) and by far prefer beer or wine.

This type of "drinking history" is quite common in the old country and would work in the US as well. We raised our son here and let him have the occasional glass of wine or beer as a teenager, possibly committing a felony along the way. As a consequence, he did not drink excessively as a student away from home nor now as an adult.

By taking the flair of tasting forbidden fruit away from alcohol early and by teaching young people to drink responsibly, many problems can be avoided. Such an approach, however, requires parents to actually educate their children instead of delegating this task completely to the school.

And finally, does it really seem logical to allow an eighteen-year old to die for his or her country, but to deny him or her a drink to celebrate having gotten away alive?

Economic Strategy

To the simple-minded non-economist, there seem to be two obvious categories of economy. The first, usually dictated by necessity, is that of developing countries with natural resources, but without the technology to convert these to high-value goods. Many African and quite a few Latin American nations find themselves in the unfortunate situation of having to export their valuable timber, ore and oil often at rock-bottom prices to industrialized countries, which then add value through their sophisticated manufacturing and export the finished goods with substantial profits, amongst others back to the third world.

The second category comprises these developed countries, which reap the benefit of having heavily invested in research and development to establish the valuable refining capabilities. Germany is a good example for that: Without significant natural resources, it was more or less forced to come up with high-quality and innovative manufacturing so advanced that despite the strong European currency it continues to be a (presently even the) leading exporter of the world. The country's GDP grew by 1.5% during the first quarter of 2008, and its manufacturing companies' order books were full until the end of 2009, before the ongoing global recession changed the world.

During the last decade(s), however, a third category has surfaced, consisting so far of only one nation – a nation blessed with both: rich in natural resources and long known for its ingenuity and leading in high technology in many fields. Amazingly, its government seems to have decided voluntarily to move the economy back towards that of a developing country. It exploits its old growth forests to export lumber to industrialized nations like Japan and seafood and agricultural products to booming South East Asia, while it imports countless value-added goods from consumer electronics to airplanes (the latter even from Brazil, by many still considered an – albeit rapidly – developing country). The simple-minded non-economist is left baffled: Why on earth would one of the few countries that have it all pursue this strategy, let valuable know-how become obsolete, destroy hundreds of thousands of skilled jobs, run up a huge trade deficit in the process and turn itself into a distributor of products manufactured elsewhere?

I am sure any highly educated economist would have the answer. Maybe it would involve increasing profit margins, shareholder value and executive salaries of the domestic corporations, which – if they are really astute – have already moved their headquarters to an offshore island to avoid taxes in their homeland. Or maybe it's just an act of charity: Allow the rest of the world to catch up, and hope for it eventually to return the favor. Either does not make much sense to me, but then I am neither an economist nor a politician with their far-sighted wisdom.

Elite

If anybody, then many of the Founding Fathers and Framers in their time deserved the label "elitist". They were successful businessmen and landowners, and often highly educated and well-versed in science, philosophy or the law. Advanced education was considered an asset then, and I doubt very much that The Declaration of Independence, the US Constitution or The Bill of Rights could have been written by a hockey mom proud of her mediocrity.

The high esteem for education still holds true for many parts of the world, notably Asia – that is why today Asian-Americans outnumber students of other ethnic origin at many of America's top universities. So the brush-clearing, football-watching, anti-intellectual president may soon be a memory of the past – not a bad development, if America wants to remain a main player in an increasingly sophisticated New World, where folksy may be nice but not enough to be successful and a respected leader.

If I were to vote (thus delegating life-and-death decisions potentially directly affecting me to someone else), I would want this to be a person at least as intelligent and educated as myself, and preferably more so. At the risk of sounding elitist, I would not select our plumber (whose handiwork I highly respect) or a pitbull with lipstick.

EMOTIONAL DISPLAYS

Our generation was trained not to display emotions in public. Feelings were a personal and very private matter and nobody else's business – an obvious cultural difference between Europe and the Near East, where at funerals public wailing and massive demonstrations of sorrow are customary and expected.

Curiously, in today's United States personal feelings are also often shared with a large audience. There is hardly a local news cast without friends or relatives of a murder victim declaring in tears what a fine human being was needlessly lost. Even when closure was only reached after decades, the grandchildren frequently cannot help but sob on prime time.

These emotions in most cases are certainly honest, but is it appropriate and does it help to show them on TV for the world to see? This is not the much-maligned media's fault, as it takes two for an interview to happen. If the victim of a tragedy wants to be left alone or in the company of a few caring friends, no reporter would be allowed in. For me it is difficult to understand, why anybody in times of sadness would search the limelight – or why there would be a rubber-necking audience eager to watch.

Equally amazing are some of the public displays of happiness, when young couples seem to be unable to let go of each other, to the delight of sympathetic spectators. Interestingly, the more intense the demonstrations of affections are, the shorter the marriages seem to last.

Maybe genuine deep feelings are still best kept from the public eye.

Euro

From the beginning of the outgoing administration, European countries became the target of constant ridicule. Their economies were in tatters, as citizens were tightening their purse strings, while that of the US was roaring ahead thanks to unfaltering consumer spending. The Euro dropped more than 10% in value against the dollar right after its introduction, and unemployment was soaring. In fact, the "old countries" were history, and if they were not supporting the US in its war on Iraq, America would go it alone (So bragged the president – Who was not with him, was against him). Worst of all was France (Remember Freedom Fries?): After being liberated from the Nazis, they should have felt obliged to follow wherever the US saw fit to lead.

How much difference a few years can make. The Euro has increased significantly in value, while the dollar has been sliding into never before seen depths against many major currencies. The American house of credit cards was crumbling, as German companies were exporting more than ever despite the strong Euro. Unemployment is on the rise here and steadily falling in Germany, and even the miserable socialist healthcare in Europe might not look so bad to the more than 40 million uninsured Americans.

Although this is a development worrisome to us here, it isn't all bad. It made think people about alternative energy sources, conserving and recycling, smaller and more fuel-efficient cars and, yes, even about saving rather than spending. American Diplomacy is no longer an oxymoron, but the dominant hawks are grudgingly admitting that negotiations are sometimes more effective (and a lot less costly) than bombs. This country's President-Elect (Bless his heart) even dared to admit that the most powerful nation in the world cannot solve all problems alone but needs the help of others.

Funny, how this change in attitude is reflected in our daily lives. Fries are French again, and "Euro" is no longer an insult – quite the opposite. TV commercials advertise EuroDeluxe beds with Eurotops and disinfectants leaving your Euro-toilet Euro-clean - and Euro-design for anything from women's dresses to furniture is in. Even "Euro-inspired" is a plus, and "Old World Charm" shows up again in American travel brochures.

The truth of course is somewhere in the middle. There is not only the American and the wrong Way of responding to challenges, as not everything in or coming from Germany is better (which some of our local compatriots seem to think. Why then are they here?). What we need to do is to recognize our weaknesses and the other side's strengths and assimilate the latter; then let anybody try to stop us. Learning from each other is of particular importance during this time of global interconnection, when grave mistakes made by one big economy can impact the whole world. Just look at the mess we are in now...

EVOLUTION

Evolution has become a hot topic – even (and particularly) amongst those completely unencumbered by scientific knowledge. This is especially true for the U.S. – in Europe the better basic education has long made it a non-issue. Like their highly educated clerics, devout Christians do not see a conflict between the figurative speech of the bible and well-established facts, and the designer is acknowledged as even more intelligent for having laid out the complex plan the world has pursued since conception. I have yet to find anybody outside this country, who believes that Adam and Eve, dinosaurs, the Orion nebula and Valencia oranges were created within the same week a few thousand years ago. For the rest of the world, the most important fact evolution teaches us is that we are and live in just a snapshot of a vast chain of events.

In my field of biology, for centuries scientists have tried to catch this snapshot by slapping labels on zillions of living organisms, to be able to file them away in the appropriate drawer named species, genus, family and so on. Passionate discussions have been (and still are) going on between "splitters" and "lumpers", but when the dust will finally settle, evolution may already have made the agreement obsolete. The invention by German taxonomists of "*Kleinarten*" (between species and subspecies) and other crutches cannot conceal that organisms are in flux and continuously manifest themselves as new hybridogenic or mutagenic species, while we are still arguing about how best to label their parents.

Even the much heralded DNA diagnostics can identify "cryptic" species, but does not tell us how to classify them in our rigid scheme.

So whether you are a creationist who just does not "believe" in evolution (Sorry, but you are simply uneducated and probably also don't "believe" in black holes, the Big Bang and many other phenomenona you cannot find in the bible) or a taxonomist struggling with the bewildering multitude of life forms not fitting into you clear-cut scheme – just accept that while it is a worthwhile endeavor to try to bring human order into the universe, we (snapshots ourselves) might just not be up to the challenge. At that scale, it simply does not matter, whether you assign a plant to Scrophulariaceae or Plantaginaceae.

And never assume that what is not supposed to exist (according to the textbooks or the bible) does not – it most likely does. Your Intelligent Designer, Mother Nature or whomever you choose to give credit to far exceeds your wildest imagination and beliefs.

F

This "F" does not stand for the dreaded f-word, but for the failing grade the outgoing US administration so richly deserves. Just look at the accomplishments over eight years of a president, who values ideology more than the well-being of the country and its people, together with his administration selected for loyalty rather than competence, and supported by a congress with the generally accepted pet-name "Do-Nothing-".

The list of major problems this president was confronted with from the beginning of his first term was all but overwhelming and still is. Social Security will be running out of money, health insurance is unaffordable for tens of millions of Americans, illegal immigration is rampant with 10-12 million undocumented immigrants already in the country, climate change and global warming are being ignored (while dependence on foreign oil continues to increase), the environment is continuously degraded by urban sprawl and the undermining of clean air and water regulations as well as attempts to revoke the Endangered Species Act, the country's infrastructure is crumbling from bridges to highways to levees and dams, public transportation is non-existing in many parts of the country (thus further damaging the environment and increasing our foreign oil addiction), the budget and trade deficits are astronomical resulting in a weakened dollar – the list goes on and on.

As if these inherited problems were not enough, the past eight years added more. The US were attacked by vicious fanatics resulting in a war on terrorists and the country that harbored them (Afghanistan), the climate change demanded acceleration of the search for clean alternative energy, and the real estate bubble burst proving that even in a free market you cannot expect profit-oriented companies to regulate themselves.

So which of this multitude of problems was solved by the president, his administration and Congress in the course of eight years? The answer is easy – none, zero, zilch. The instigator of the 2001 terrorist attack is still at large, since the war in Afghanistan was neglected for a hugely expensive one on a country that was never a threat to the US, but after its almost complete destruction now became a new haven for terrorists. Universal healthcare is still a dream, illegal immigration still alive and well, infrastructure and environment are in worse shape than eight years ago, and the favorite solution for global warming would be drilling for more oil.

Instead, the legislature addressed burning problems such as steroid use by baseball players, the continuation of life support beyond many years for a poor woman in Florida, the legal standing of a Cuban boy after his arrival in Miami, and whether gays should be allowed to marry or burning the flag is a felony. This Congress was actually proud to announce the signing into law several of the recommendations made by the 9/11 Committee – after three (3) years of bickering. The executive meanwhile managed to insult even the country's staunchest allies by megalomaniac arrogance.

The United States were founded by highly educated and strongly committed revolutionaries (not Joe Sixpack), and grew to dominating strength through the hard work of generations of immigrants and their offspring. Surely future generations deserve a better inheritance than what this one has prepared so far.

May the next president be able to assemble a team of competent bipartisan coworkers and be lucky enough to partner with an equally capable Congress. Lack of experience with the present system of inefficient mismanagement could be a plus. As should be his mixed race, multicultural background (This country has always been successful as a melting pot of people of different origin and race) and popularity abroad, since replacing diplomacy with arrogance and bombs does not seem to have been all that great. But then what did you expect from a president, whose main qualifications for the job were a DUI arrest, avoiding military service and bankrupting an oil company?

FREE MARKET

As perceived by many, one of the cornerstones of our democratic system is a "Free Market", unimpeded by government regulations and bureaucratic red tape. Competition is healthy, consumers are the selective force enabling the fittest to survive, and everybody wins. So goes the theory; reality tends to differ.

First of all, the top priority for any corporation, large or small, is not to police itself, but to maximize profits and shareholder value. If they are ethical (as most of them are), that happens within the law and the many loopholes it provides; if they are not, the gray area gets extended well into the dark side.

One of the results is that many manufacturing jobs are being exported to low-wage countries (Have you seen "Manufactured in China, assembled in Mexico", distributed with pride in the US?), and the service industry follows closely behind (Ever encountered the phone Customer Service rep named John or Sally, with a heavy Indian accent?). All in the name of healthy competition, driven by the customer who above all wants cheap, cheaper, cheapest.

Surprisingly some of the most ardent advocates of the concept now mourn the loss of jobs (including maybe their own), the complete disappearance of manufacturing know-how (Try to buy a TV built in the US), and the lack of product quality and even safety. Which reminds me of "The Apprentice" (Goethe's, not The

Donald's), who cannot get rid of the spirits he called: *"Die ich rief, die Geister, werd ich nun nicht los!"*.

This is unfortunately one of the flaws of democracy – you get what you wish (vote) for, and any democratic country has the government it elected based on the candidates' platform (hopefully). So don't complain, but vote better next time…

(Thank you. You have.)

FRIENDS

I have yet to hear an American talk about acquaintances. Nobody seems to have them but only friends - usually scores, and if you include those on myspace.com, hundreds. I could probably count mine by the fingers of my hands and, strangely enough, feel blessed not deprived. I also like and appreciate the many acquaintances I have made personally and professionally, but would never call them friends. So what's the difference, completely ignored in this society?

A German proverb (There are German proverbs for all and any occasions) states, *"Freunde in der Not gehen tausend auf ein Lot"*, which translated freely means: When you need them, a thousand friends fit into an ounce. That pretty much sums it up. A true friend is somebody to whom you can turn when you need help, to whom you can open your heart (not just your mouth) when needing advice or consolation, whom you can trust to stand by you no matter what.

Do Americans really have so many of these, or if not, what is the term for the few everybody needs and hopefully has? "Buddy" doesn't sound right, while "friend" does (It obviously has the same root as the German *"Freund"*) but misses the point. Or is the lack of differentiation between acquaintances and friends a symptom of the stereotypical American superficiality? Real friendships must have been common here during the early days, when the ability to rely on your neighbor was essential for survival in an unknown and often hostile environment. Did friendship get lost as so many other virtues of the pioneer times? Do people these days feel safer closing up than opening up?

Let's hope not. Permanently replacing a few friends with many "friends" would be a sad development of humanity.

Fundamentalism

Islamic fundamentalists are a scary bunch. How can one comprehend people, who are convinced they have found the only truth, want to impose their belief on the whole world, and do not distance themselves even from violence as a means to accomplish this goal? Islam is understood by most Moslems to be a peaceful religion; so how can it give rise to such uncompromising fanaticism?

For an answer, just look back into the history of Christianity: the Spanish inquisition, the crusades, the conquest of Latin America by the conquistadores – better dead than alive as a heathen. Nor were the Salem witch trials an example of religious tolerance, but if you prefer the present, how about America's "Religious Right"? Yelling demonstrators with hateful posters and the occasional bombing of a clinic or the assassination of a doctor are not exactly a pretty picture, either. Anything is more humane than Shariah Law, but is it truly civilized to force a woman to carry out a baby conceived from a rapist, or one that may kill her during birth? To value a morula in a Petri dish more highly than the search for a cure for millions of sufferers from accidents or presently incurable diseases? Or to be uneducated enough not to "believe" in evolution in spite of overwhelming evidence, while (usually highly educated) clerics and theologians of all major religions have no problem to reconcilliate science with ancient scriptures? On the other hand, listening to a home schooling parent in the

21st century ("Yes, we teach our children about evolution, but we also tell them the truth") gives me the shivers – Is this where America is going?

Of course we rightly condemn a regime that supports terrorism and encourages people to commit mass murder of innocents by blowing themselves up. But is the best response for a super-power to bomb the hell out of such a country, resulting in countless more deaths?

Any religion can be abused as a pretext for intolerance and violence towards non-believers (infidels) and then become a major component in brutal wars everywhere – Ireland, the Balkans, the Near East, Darfur, Indonesia, you name it. In all cases, lack of factual education and its replacement with indoctrination is probably the main culprit. In my opinion there is no right or wrong way to practice religion. If there is a personalized almighty and omniscient God, as many firmly believe but nobody knows for sure, He (She, It) is highly unlikely to frown upon a human being trying to live a decent life, but belonging to the "wrong" church. Such a God surely does not need middle management to interpret her (his, its) will, and probably won't look too kindly on commanders-in-chief deciding that tens of thousands of people are better off dead than living under a dictator.

GENDER AND RACE

America has come a long way since we arrived here in the early seventies, when a white colleague of mine at NIH still had to struggle to have his black wife accepted in the community pool of the development they called home, and when a secretary was of course female and the boss male. These days, a little more than a generation later, I have worked with female bosses and their male administrative assistants (There are no more secretaries except in the government, where they are spelt with a capital S and very important), and a woman and an African-American (There are no more black people in this country) were the finalists in the race to become the Democratic candidate for the presidency of the United States.

So finally things are the way they ought to be: Gender is no longer an issue (as it isn't in numerous other countries, where the state's highest office is held by women, my home country included), and skin color surely doesn't matter, as was shown in the Democratic primaries, when the (half) black candidate secured the majority of the white vote in several states. Only the political platform, the competency and the personalities of the candidates will determine, who will be elected the next leader of the free world – wouldn't that be nice.

Unfortunately, there are still major obstacles to be overcome on the way to true equality. For one, there are the professional African-Americans, who never cease to search for evidence of discrimination. In a recent TV interview, I actually heard one of these gentlemen discount polls that 80% of the voters claimed that race does not matter to them, since exit polls showed that in reality 10-15% are biased against non-whites. Unless my math is wrong, I can't see a discrepancy there – so let the fossils vote color. Then there are the myopic feminists, seemingly unable to see anything but gender, who threaten to vote Republican, since their favorite female Democratic candidate came in second. Out of spite, I guess, since war, healthcare, taxes and other issues don't seem to matter – nor the fact that the Republican candidate is also male. And finally, there are the much-maligned "mass media". From voting analyses to random (?) interviews, they rarely miss an opportunity to remind the viewer/reader of the influence race and gender might have

So, American voter, please focus on the issues, vote your conscience, and ignore gender and race. Make sure the next POTUS represents the country you are proud of the way you want it to be seen, and addresses the many grave problems the way you want them resolved.

(After having written this, my worry about "myopic feminists" seemed to be justified: Sarah Palin's nomination for Vice President provided a major bounce to the Republican ticket in polls, mainly due to white women valuing a woman, any woman even as VP more than all the major issues combined in the presidential candidates' programs. According to Palin, these women all of a sudden believed the Iraq war is God's will (as is another pipeline across Alaska), that Climate Change and Global Warming are a myth, that abortions should be outlawed even for rape and incest victims, and, and, and.

Fortunately I was proven wrong concluding that hockey moms were in the process of displaying their inability to grasp problems and commit to their solution. Their initial emotional frustration soon gave way to making a rational choice after all.

Am I glad I was wrong…)

GOP

This abbreviation, I learnt despite the ear-deafening noise produced by the religious right, does not stand for "God's Own Party". Now that I know, old it is, but what is grand about it to justify the *über-alles* claim made by some of its supporters?

First of all, I thought, came protecting the individual from undue interference by a big federal government. Wrong, I found out – the Republican president supported by a then Republican Congress installed Big Brother surveillance even without court orders as particularly patriotic. And the two million government members and employees don't seem to mind the excellent healthcare plan provided by the otherwise much-maligned federal government. At least they allow ordinary taxpayers, who are not eligible to participate, to foot 80% of the bill.

One of the Founding Fathers' most important principle was the separation of church and state. Many of them were highly educated businessmen and scientists and saw religion as a personal matter, not one to be propagated by the government. Compare that to the present president, who claims God as his personal consultant, considers Intelligent Design as a topic to be taught in public schools, and displays his own level of education just about every time he gives a speech.

Another ideal was letting into the country the poor and persecuted of the world, while keeping out the bad guys. Come on, the best a Republican president could think of was building a triple fence rather than enforcing the law? I guess there are already enough poor citizens in the country...

And how about fiscal responsibility? A great Republican president (has he been canonized yet?) left a budget deficit behind that took his democratic successor two terms to fix, and the present not so great one will leave a mountain of debt behind for generations to struggle with.

So when I read about the GOP and its early presidents, I find myself quite close to their ideals and actions. But today? I'd much rather be called a – gosh – liberal (not bleeding-heart though) than a follower of the party that was once grand. When the Republican Party will no longer be represented by a good old boys club approving each others' earmarks and giving tax breaks to the similarly wealthy but will rediscover its old ideals, it may actually deserve those three letters again.

GUNS

Guns save lives? The statistics are irrefutable: In countries with strict gun control laws such as Canada, Japan and most of Europe, a lot fewer people become innocent victims of crimes committed with firearms. Which contradicts one of the gun lovers' favorite claims that if only criminals had guns, they would reap havoc on defenseless law-abiding citizens. In fact, seldom are guns used in self-defense (I don't count the Texas murderer who on purpose killed two burglars by shooting them in the back as a "defendant"), but much more often by an irate family member or acquaintance to settle an irrelevant argument, defeating another of the NRA's favorite slogans: "Guns don't kill, people do". What kills are *people with guns*, as pulling the trigger is so much easier than sticking a knife into a fellow human being's body. In fact, guns often create criminals during family disputes, barroom brawls or road incidents by turning previously law-abiding citizens into enraged killers.

So what is the reason for America's unwavering fascination with guns? That even a mass murder at a college does not cure, but instead leads to the demand by some for college teachers and students to bring weapons of their own, presumably to liven up boring academic lectures with an occasional shoot-out. It can't be the obsolete constitutional right to bear arms, which only allows but does not require you to do so. Are guns an indispensable accessory to lift the self-confidence of otherwise insecure would-be cowboys? Or is it for sport, from target shooting in a gun club to hitting beer cans and, much more fun, traffic signs in the desert? Or are many gun owners so afraid (paranoid) that they need the comfort of a hand gun in their night stand drawer?

I may never find out, but the thousands of innocent gun victims every year (more than 12,000 killed outright, almost 53,000 treated in emergency rooms for gunshot wounds) seem too stiff a price to pay for the right of firearm aficionados to continue cuddling their babies. Compare this to Canada (latest annual toll of gun deaths: 168) or Great Britain (about 100) – and if you think you need a gun to defend your family, keep in mind that every day in the US eight children die from gun shot wounds.

Could strict gun control laws be introduced in this country, with 300 million firearms in private hands (one for every citizen)? Australia set an example in 1996 with the result that the rate of gun deaths has fallen by half. Today, Australia has per capita a gun-crime rate less than one-tenth of that in the United States. I guess Aussies don't have a NRA, and a parliament less subservient to lobbyists.

HEROES

Nowhere in the world could it be easier to be a hero than in America. The moment you put on a uniform (unless it's a bellboy's) you are practically destined to become one.

The old-fashioned definition of a hero is somebody who is aware of grave danger, but takes the risk anyway to help someone in need (Taking a risk without realizing the danger is not heroic but stupid.). Examples for true heroism are not uncommon here or elsewhere: The unknown survivor of a plane crash diving into the freezing waters of the Potomac to save fellow passengers until he himself disappears; the New Yorker risking his life to pull a fallen pedestrian from the subway tracks right in front of a speeding train; the motorist freeing a trapped driver from his burning vehicle; the Morgan Stanley employee supervising the evacuation of 2,000 coworkers from the burning North Tower (to then perish during his attempt to save more) – and of course the firefighter breaking into a house engulfed in flames to rescue its inhabitants, or the soldier risking his life to aid an injured comrade.

But look who else is being celebrated. An elementary school teacher revered by her students is a role model, not a hero. The police officer who is run over by a drunk driver or shot by a criminal is not a hero but a victim. The soldier making a wrong turn in a war zone and taken prisoner by the enemy is not even that but rather less than competent. Even the poor souls on flight

UA 93, who tried to overwhelm their highjackers, were not heroes attempting to save others than themselves, but innocent victims of fanatic killers.

Many good people are Samaritans or benefactors helping fellow human beings in trouble without being (or expecting to be called) heroes; so let's reserve this epithet for those who truly deserve it. Then even in this country of superlatives there will no longer be a need to coin new terms like the recently invented "super-hero". And weekly magazines may no longer invite you to purchase gift subscriptions to become a Holiday Hero…

HIGH TECHNOLOGY

America has always been at the forefront of innovation in science and engineering, as is readily confirmed by the number of Nobel Prizes in medicine and chemistry awarded to its pioneers, its accomplishments in space exploration or the sophistication of its war machines, to name a few examples.

But then there are toll booths, where high volume freeway traffic comes to a grinding halt to allow drivers to throw coins into baskets, or to obtain tickets from a human being sitting all day in said booth, with nothing else to do but handing out little pieces of paper.

Or how about trained pharmacists opening original drug packages to count the number of pills placed there by a fully automated machine, to then fill them into a different plastic container with a newly typed label – all while the customer has to wait for twenty minutes instead of simply receiving a package off the shelf.

The ultimate embarrassment, however, must be voting. No other civilized country in the world seems to have the problems regularly encountered in the cradle of democracy, from hanging chads to malfunctioning computers to lost registrations or delayed mail-ins. Maybe one day the government could borrow the NASA team of Mars Rover engineers to master the formidable task of receiving, counting and documenting poll results every couple of years…

HOME SCHOOLING

Extreme religious groups favor it as an alternative to the "secular indoctrination" in public schools, and it scares me a lot, considering how deficient even the latter often is. How much math, history and geography can the average mother or father teach?

I certainly would be in no position to explain trigonometry, integrals and differential calculations to a teenager, and even the basics of mundane geography would require substantial preparation on my side (Where is Tadjikistan? Where the source of the Nile? What is the capital of Slovenia? That of Slovakia?). I would not be much better off in History: The cause of the 30 Year War? The 100 Year War? What about the Irish famine and the fate of the Huguenots (both of which had quite an impact on American history)? Or to stay even more local – Who were Cabrillo, Junipero Serra, Father Kino?

Thanks to my background in science, I would feel comfortable discussing the fossil record and the methods of dating it, molecular genetics and sequence homologies between man and other primates, evolution and climate change – but would you?

And we have not even addressed foreign languages, although at least some rudimentary knowledge of for instance French or Spanish would be an asset in trying to communicate with America's direct neighbors.

Is all that included in a home schooling curriculum, or is it considered unimportant since not in the bible?

HOMO SAPIENS

Almost 300 years ago, Linnaeus named our species "wise", and one wonders whether he would have chosen the same adjective today - or would he now prefer *Homo callidus*? Since smart we undoubtedly are, more so than any other living organism on earth; but wise?

No other animal (except maybe certain ants – not desirable company) spends a substantial portion of its resources on devising ever better means to destroy large numbers of its own kind. Another significant amount of our ingenuity and energy is applied to exploiting our natural habitat all the way to its utter destruction. Both activities in turn lead to more expenditure for attempts to cancel out the results of these efforts (through defense and reclamation). It is our smartness that allows us to pursue these goals with increasing effectivity; wisdom would keep us from setting them in the first place.

We have learnt to drain wetlands, level mesas, fill canyons and clear-cut forests, and practice these skills relentlessly. Evolution has always had to cope with changes, but at a very different pace. New and more efficient predators led to better defense mechanisms in their prey (evasion, camouflage, armor, etc.). Climatic changes usually allowed organisms to develop protection or to find refuge in a more suitable environment. The precipitous changes triggered by our species, however, leave the victims no time to adapt, with an increasing rate of extinction of plant and animal species as the result.

So is mankind destined to become as catastrophic an event for the rest of the world as the impact of a meteor, alleged to have wiped out countless species? Will we become our own undoing as a dead end of evolution like the dinosaurs ("Too much armor, too little brain")? Or is there hope that our adolescent smartness will develop into mature wisdom in time?

The politics of many Old World countries have turned greener over the past decades, but let's face it – only after much worth protecting had already been lost (Think of the forests of the Mediterranean or the large predators and their prey in central Europe). The United States would be in a better position and looked promising just a few years ago, when polluted rivers were cleaned up and old growth forests and fragile desert habitats were protected at a significant scale. Since then, however, the pendulum has swung in the other direction, and all that seems to matter now is economic growth at any price, and a military build-up to protect the country against perceived threats (and to spread the blessings of the American Way of Life to whomever seems to be in need of conversion). The commitment to preserving the natural riches and the beauty of the country, on the other hand, is comparable to the strategic vision of a public company: As long as the next quarterly report looks good, who cares. Of course there is always hope, but would it not be great, if there were more than just that?

Until then, hop into your V8 SUV to drive to the supermarket (Who needs public transportation?) and enjoy the unlimited supply of oil, by your personal version of the Almighty created for you to burn. Don't bother to sort your garbage (Recycling is truly a nuisance), and ignore those bothersome nay-Sayers; China and India pollute just as much. Global Warming requires more study anyway, and the (sea to) shining sea looks most beautiful with an oil slick in the distance. .

HOMOSEXUALITY

This should like any sexuality be a very personal and private matter; gay pride parades and similar public demonstrations of one's preference are only embarrassing. I find anything acceptable that happens between consenting adult human beings, but save me the noisy display of your particular inclination.

Homosexuality is not normal (If it were the norm, mankind would have gone extinct a long time ago), but it is certainly not unnatural, either. It happens between mammals from dolphins to chimpanzees, in birds from geese to penguins, and even frogs and toads practice it occasionally – usually for lack of other opportunity, but sometimes even in its presence.

Gay and lesbian partners with the appropriate commitment deserve the same legal treatment as any other couple, and their union should be accepted and respected by society. With that accomplished, any fight for the label "marriage" seems inappropriate. This term has always been applied to the bond between man and woman, and should remain reserved for it. The insistence that from now on blue should be called green does not change the color – it just confuses matters and in addition makes the proponents of the change look rather ridiculous.

HUMOR

As many Americans will be happy to explain to you, Germans are dead-serious people devoid of any sense of humor. Interestingly, Germans are equally certain that Americans are humorless, but both groups are in accordance that the British are really strange in this respect.

Of course both sides are wrong – Americans as well as Germans fortunately have a pronounced sense of humor, but boy, is it different. Having switched back and forth frequently between both countries, that was one of my first lessons to learn. Joking with my American secretary – sorry, Administrative Assistant - the same way I did with my German one would have landed me in jail or at least in re-education for political correctness by the local Human Resources office. Interacting the American professional way with my German associate would have resulted in a reprimand from her ("If you don't tease me, I can't tease you back – so where's the fun?").

German humor often involves subtle irony or even sarcasm Americans mostly do not understand. After taking my first job in the US (a postdoctoral position at a highly sophisticated Ivory League university), I was shocked to realize that my new colleagues took my silly remarks seriously (You bet I changed really fast). American humor on the other hand is frequently in-your-face slapstick, no reading between the lines necessary. A particular incarnation is propagated by stand-up comics on channel TV, where the sole mentioning of private parts or banned four-letter f-, s-, c- etc words is usually rewarded with roars of laughter from the grateful audience.

So whatever your preference may be – sense of humor seems to be an acquired taste, and don't assume others don't have any just because it differs from yours.

HUNTING

Hunting is a sport, they say.

I always thought sport is synonymous with fairness, a competition between participants with equal chances to win; that's why doping is prohibited. So where is the sportsmanship, when a hunter in camouflage gear with a high-powered rifle aims at a deer browsing peacefully in a forest clearing? Of course that is better than shooting fenced-in zoo animals at a Texas game ranch, but fair sport? Give me a break. If you just enjoy the thrill of successfully stalking a wary animal with senses superior to yours, maybe you could emulate the catch-and-release fishermen and use paintballs instead of bullets? A careless moose or deer with pink or light blue blotches might be embarrassed but much better off than dead.

Subsistence hunting is of course different. You don't have to be an Inuit in Alaska or an Indian in the Brazilian rainforest to qualify for an exception – the farmer in West Virginia who wants to put meat on the family table does, too. But killing just for fun or a trophy for your den does not make you a sportsman by any stretch of the imagination.

IMMIGRATION

Being an immigrant myself, I feel justified to voice a few thoughts on this issue. While I was considered to be a "person of distinguished merit" able to fill positions no qualified Americans could be found for, it took years of often degrading treatment by the INS (now under a different acronym part of Homeland Security) finally to be admitted as a then (no longer) permanent resident. It is therefore easy for me to imagine what an unskilled Mexican farm worker would have to go through to immigrate legally. The result (8 or 10 or 12, who knows, million illegal, pardon – non-documented aliens) comes as no surprise.

So what could Congress do about it, if it were a working institution? First (yes, first – minutemen, presidential candidates and others pandering to the conservative base are wrong about that) make legal immigration easy. Give out 3 or 5 year work permits and require legal immigrants to get a (any) job within 6 months, pay taxes including Social Security and Medicare, and let them find permanent employment during the following years, during which they could also apply for residency. If they don't succeed, send them back and make sure they stay there. To guarantee that, close the border – not with a fence ("Build a 20 ft fence, and I'll show you a 22 ft ladder") ruining the environment, but with electronic surveillance, the gear for which can probably be acquired inexpensively from an industrialized nation like

China. Make sure the Border Patrol has enough manpower and equipment to follow through.

And the Illegals already here? No amnesty, and no deportation with all its hardships either. Give them 3 months to register with Homeland Security, and put them on the same track as new legal immigrants (see above), plus an additional reasonable (!) fine for their unlawful immigration. Who does not register, gets deported, hardship or not. Any employer of unregistered aliens needs to face (very) stiff penalties. This approach would prevent damage to our economy (which in many areas depends on migrant or established non-documented workers), would allow anybody to move out of the shadow, and should satisfy hawks and doves.

Does this sound too easy? It probably is, since otherwise our hard-working and competent senators and congress men and women would have come up with it a long time ago. So, Honorable Representatives, show me the flaws, fix them (You are paid quite well for that) and get it done. Get it finally done. Or have "effective legislature" and "efficient executive" become oxymoron in this country? A congress preferring to deal with baseball steroids and individuals on life-support rather than immigration (or universal healthcare, social security, preemptive wars, economic crises, the education debacle, etc.) unfortunately doesn't bode well.

While these changes are being made and implemented, the US should also have intensive discussions with the Mexican president, who has to show serious efforts to make his country more attractive to its citizens, so that they don't want to leave in drones. That mainly means creating living-wage jobs, an approach with which the US could even be helpful. Mr. Bush has often stated that he wants to fight terrorists abroad rather than in this country – maybe a similar strategy could be applied to illegal immigration...

KATRINA

Much has been said and written about the nightmare named Katrina, and rightly so. The amount of suffering and hardship it has brought upon hundreds of thousands of people defies description and is arguably one of the worst the United States of America have ever experienced as a consequence of a natural disaster. In its aftermath, I cannot help but dream how things should have developed instead.

During the week of increasingly dire warnings about the monster hurricane approaching the gulf coast, the richest and most powerful country in the world have readied itself for the onslaught. Military and National Guard were mobilized and on red alert. Airplanes, helicopters and trucks in all adjacent states were loaded with drinking water, MREs, clothes, cots, tents, generators and all the other anticipated necessities, all ready to be dropped (parachuted) into disaster areas. When the mandatory evacuation order for New Orleans was issued, hundreds of buses and ambulances streamed into the city, to pick up the poor and the sick unable to leave on their own. Katrina then devastated an empty city, with substantial material damage but no or little loss of human life. And when the levees finally gave way (as predicted for months and years by countless computer models), the Corps of Engineers was ready with equipment and supplies to close the breaches as fast as humanly possible and to start pumping out the flood waters.

An even less realistic dream goes along these lines. Years ago, when it was concluded that New Orleans' levees could only withstand category 3 hurricanes and that eventually the city's luck would run out, the local and Federal governments bit the bullet and spent billions of dollars to strengthen the protective dams for the inevitable category 5 storm. While this action would undoubtedly have strained the country, the US would probably have been able to match similar efforts by other superpowers (such as The Netherlands). It would, however, have required know-how possibly not available to administrations at the time – such as, "A Stitch in Time Saves Nine", or "Prevention is better than Therapy".

After Katrina, the US would then have gratefully acknowledged the offers of help pouring in even from some of the world's poorest countries hit by last year's killer tsunami, but gracefully declined, since the country had the means and resources to stage a virtual invasion of the affected areas for a spectacular search, rescue and rebuilding effort. The rest of the world would have looked with envy at this shining example of well-applied power and care, and all Americans would have lived happily ever after.

So much for the dreams. Reality as we know was very different. It took four days of thirst, hunger and in many cases unnecessary death for the first significant help shipments to arrive. During this time, the situation in New Orleans developed similarities to that in liberated Baghdad: looting, rapes, murders and sniper attacks on security forces – which may have confirmed to many Iraqi people that this is the kind of democracy they were getting from America. But there were fortunately also positive developments. It took congress in the face of a national tragedy only four days to convene (For comparison: To pass a law trying to prevent the removal of Ms. Schiavo's feeding tube took a few hours even on a holiday), and the President of the country actually flew low over the stricken areas to show his heartfelt support. Thanks to that spectacular demonstration, the United States of America may in the future no longer have to wage war to spread their form of democracy, but the peoples of the world may just stand in line to adopt it.

KNOW-IT-ALLS

You have run into them, professionally and privately – these lovable contemporaries who simply know everything. They are usually easy to spot right-away, since they cannot wait to share their wealth of knowledge. In any conversation or discussion they don't listen (never having acquired that skill), but only wait for a break to interject what they ware burning to say. If they listen at all to specialists in a given field, then only to get a confirmation of what they already know; any differing comments are ignored. I have traded e-mails with one of them, who in his replies would take my text and insert his valuable comments in a different color even in the middle of my sentences. How much fun it would be to talk with this gentleman... (I have successfully avoided that up to now).

I have met a person who never had a dog in her life, but read an article on the internet and then felt the urge to explained dog psychology to me (I was raised with dogs). A former coworker of mine, who had spent a grand total of one (1) week outside the US on a business trip to Belgium, subsequently taught me the differences between European and American culture and society (I have lived 30 years on each of these continents). A friend of ours spent two or three days on a business trip in New Zealand and told us afterwards "These are tiny islands with nothing to see" (We spent a month there and barely scratched the surface of this gorgeous country's natural wonders). Other friends had traveled "all over" Puerto Rico (in 4 days) and judged the island not worth a visit; we loved it after 3 weeks (short even for a superficial acquaintance). My childless sister-in-law reprimanded me for the mistakes I was making raising our son (who despite my shortcomings became a successful professional with his own family). A physicist and self-styled botanist lectured me about ecology and evolution, since I was obviously "immature and lacked any understanding of biological systems" (I am a molecular biologist with more than 30 years of experience in basic and applied research).

So what is wrong with me and you? Are we just awfully slow and don't get much of anything, or do we simply require more than a cursory look to come up with a final judgment on people, countries and intellectual concepts? Whatever the reason, I am very content with my limitations, as they allow me to learn something new every day, which keeps life interesting and me young (or immature, if you prefer). Should I ever know it all, I would feel terribly old, but that danger seems rather remote.

To those people with ultimate wisdom and the tendency to generously share it with us dummies, Mark Twain had some good advice, "It is better not to say anything and look stupid than to open your mouth and remove any doubt".

LANGUAGE

Globalization is affecting many aspects of our daily lives, but hardly anything more than languages. Certain German words have long been used here in the States – from difficult to translate terms such as *Gemütlichkeit, Zeitgeist* or *Angst* (the latter two are even recognized by Microsoft's Spellchecker) to scientific-technical terms (*Zwitterion* in chemistry and *Graben* in geology, to give examples) to everyday expressions like *Rucksack, Kindergarten, Wiener Schnitzel, Bratwurst* or *Gesundheit* as well as certain prefixes (*Ur-, Über-*). The converse is even more obvious, as countless English words are commonly used in German. From Computer (I don't remember, when I heard the German word *"Rechner"* the last time) to *"surfen"* and *"mailen"* (the English "to surf" and "to e-mail" turned into German verbs) to Kids for *Kinder* (children, although pronounced "kits" in the Old Country) to Sandwich (much shorter than *"Belegtes Brot"*). Germans in fact love English so much that they have invented English words only Germans can understand – *"Handy"* for cell phone for instance, or *"Beamer"* for a digital projector – similar to Spanglish, but the term "Germanglish" would be more descriptive, since it does incorporate mangling.

There is of course nothing wrong with that, although the French have tried (rather unsuccessfully) to outlaw the use of foreign words. The main purpose of language is to facilitate communication, and foreign words may make that easier. The only sad aspect of this internationalization is that hand-in-hand with it seems to go the progressive impoverishment of native languages. The active vocabulary of the average American (including the authors of popular books) pales in comparison with texts written as little as 50 or 100 years ago; the same is true for Germans. This development is accompanied by a "simplification" of grammatical rules, which has put many irregular English verbs on the Endangered List (You see more lighted candles or spoiled food than you ever dreamt of), together with "whom" (barely surviving in To Whom It May Concern) and even "an", often painfully replaced with an "a" in front of vowels. Prepositions tend to become "standardized" as well, and many people are enamored with (no longer of) replacing them by (no longer with) any coming to mind. Whether this trend is specifically American or also occurring in Great Britain I do not know, since My Fair Lady's Professor Higgins already claimed a long time ago that Americans haven't spoken English for years. I do see, however, the same tendency in German: Prepositions requiring the genitive (*"wegen des"*, *"trotz des"*) are now commonly used with the dative (That really hurts, if you know and like this language), Bavarians have long abandoned *als* in the comparative (*Eine Präposition ist einfacher wie zwei*), unusual forms of verbs are ignored (*Das bräuchte nicht zu sein*, but it becomes *"brauchte"*), and adverbs are now officially sanctioned by the Duden, the bible of German linguistics, as horrible adjectives (as in *"die zue Tür"* and *"das aufe Fenster"*, believe it or not). Small wonder then that details of spelling in both languages are considered to be rather irrelevant, too. Whether you are *zu Hause* (*hause*) or *zu Besuch* (*besuch*), don't worry about old-fashioned rules but get accustomed to *Schifffahrt* with three fs. And what's the difference between complimentary and complementary anyway?

Even worse than the frequent misspelling is the pronunciation of foreign words in both languages. Although most Germans have learnt basic English in elementary school, the trade names of household products of American origin are routinely mutilated:

Colgate becomes Kol'gahte, Wicks Vaporub 'Vahporupp", etc. French place names in the US suffer a similar fate – Lake Pontchartrain is pronounced Punch-a-train and Calais callus. There is even a book teaching how to correctly mispronounce Latin scientific plant names beyond recognition – no Roman would have understood "Highratium" to mean *Hieracium* and "Lishm" *Lycium* or "Opuncha" *Opuntia*. In all my lifelong dabbling in botany I have met one (1) American (not a botanist, but a highly knowledgeable park ranger and book author in Arizona's Kofa Mountains) who correctly pronounced Latin names – in fact, more conservatively than I ("grahkilis" rather than "grahtsilis"). Correct English pronunciation of course is a topic by itself, as already Dr. Seuss realized. Just try to explain to a poor ESL person the underlying rule for tough versus cough, slough, plough and dough, or wear versus tear (the, I mean, not to).

Does it all matter? Not really, since most people seem to understand "jacana" as well as "hacahna" and "co'yotte" as well as "'cayot". It would be nice, however, if the inherent beauty of foreign languages would be appreciated more and shine through at least occasionally. And if I as an alien with English as second language would not have had to proof-read the Ph.D. thesis of an American graduate student, to correct the countless spelling and grammatical mistakes (says I). That was then though; now I would probably have to capitulate due to my lack of familiarity with neo-Anglicisms such as jive and IMing, which may put High German and Oxford English irreversibly on the endangered species list (u just wait n c). At least I have no problem with simplified Spanish place names and can guess that TJ is Tijuana and IV Isla Vista. And why should they be better off than San Fran?

LAWYERS

The United States are arguably the most litigious country in the world, undoubtedly caused by its large number of lawyers per capita (another world record). Combine this with a system that allows lawyers to offer their services on a contingency basis and juries often known for their capricious verdicts, and you are faced with the present situation. Nobody makes mistakes any more, but is the victim of others (preferably organizations with deep pockets), who then can be sued at little or no expense to the plaintiff.

As a result, everybody tries to protect themselves against even the most unlikely liability, again of course with the help of those ubiquitous lawyers, and comes up with completely ridiculous warnings. I have bought a desk lamp carrying a label telling me not to operate it immersed in water, and walked on National Park hiking trails with a sign alerting me to the fact that I was doing this at my own risk. I was brought up with the idea that I would not only walk but LIVE at my risk, and when I got hurt doing something stupid to say, "That was stupid" and get on with it.

Here you instead seem to learn whom best to sue, when anything goes wrong. And just in case you missed an opportunity to make a quick buck that way, lawyers remind you in TV commercials that you might be entitled to financial compensation, if you or your loved ones were exposed to or suffered from whatever.

This certainly beats old-fashioned ambulance chasing, and the biggest winners in class-action lawsuits are always the law offices administering the settlements.

Small wonder then that tort reform has been a topic of discussion for many years, and will keep Congress busy talking for many more. Talking, that is.

LEGACY

In the grand picture of things, most people do not matter. Whether you and I ever lived, won't make a difference to the world, and we will simply fade away without leaving much of a trace except maybe in our immediate families and the circle of our friends. The same is true for most of today's so-called celebrities whose antics fill the tabloids, but who soon will be forgotten once their last little scandal is no longer deemed newsworthy. The exceptions of course are the giants of arts and science, whose work has made a lasting contribution to mankind's cultural heritage: painters and composers, philosophers and physicians, biologists and physicists, naturalists, benefactors and others whose names will always be remembered.

Most of us do not mind this social mortality and seem quite content with historic insignificance. Notable exceptions are the presidents of this country, who towards the end of their term show great concern about their legacy, the lasting impact their tenure will leave behind, and how they will be judged by history and future generations. This at least is one worry the 43rd does not have to have – he has managed to profoundly change the interior political landscape of this great nation and its perception around the world.

When he took over, he inherited a country with a booming economy and a projected budget surplus big enough to allow serious thoughts about finally addressing and resolving the numerous grave problems neglected by his predecessors – from a crumbling infrastructure to an unraveling social net to leaking borders and a staggering trade deficit. America was the only remaining superpower, leading in science and technology and with a solid track record of supporting human rights and civil liberties, protecting the environment and helping less fortunate nations suffering from economic woes or foreign oppression.

Then came 9/11, a brutal terrorist attack on the benevolent giant, requiring a decisive response by the supreme military power against the country that launched it, to then refocus on the burning or smoldering internal issues. Instead, the initial forceful response was abandoned before the necessary victory, a massive attack was launched on a country that was never a threat to the United States (but governed by a brutal dictator with a hugely inflated ego, similar and therefore a challenge to that of the 43rd president), and all rationality thrown into the wind. Thousands of idealistic young Americans and a hundred thousand innocent Iraqi civilians have died, hundreds ob billions of dollars have been spent (In case you forgot – that's hundreds of thousands of millions of your tax dollars), and the infrastructure and rich cultural history of one of the oldest countries in the world have been bombed and looted into oblivion.

American leadership in science and technology became a war on science reminiscent of the Dark Ages: religion determines what is right or wrong, the status quo has to be maintained above all (whether it is pills over stem cells, oil over alternative energies, creationism over evolution). Human rights succumb to torture, civil liberties to governmental power unimpeded by judicial subtleties. The best way to secure the border is not revising and enforcing immigration laws, but building a massive fence as attractive as the Berlin wall, running roughshod over existing environmental and other laws.

So the benevolent giant, who could have alleviated the worldwide disastrous consequences of tsunamis and earthquakes single-handedly, or permanently fixed most internal problems, chose instead to become the arrogant backyard bully: If you are not with me, you are against me, and we can go it alone. Don't worry, Mr. President, your legacy is secure, and future generations of Americans will not forget you, as they will struggle to pay off the bills you left them with.

LIBERATION

Liberation only works when from external oppression. Europe was grateful when liberated by the United States from Nazi-Germany's occupation, Kuwait when being freed from the Iraqi invaders. As a foreign power you can never liberate a people from its own government, however, no matter how restrictive and draconic it may be. One's own tyrants are always preferable to occupants from abroad, a lesson presently taught again in Afghanistan and repeated in Iraq.

Permanent change in a country has to come from within, by evolution or revolution, as seen throughout the world's history. Early American settlers would not have welcomed independence from the British Crown, if it had been brought and administered by the French army; it took the French themselves to get rid of their absolutistic monarchy. Cubans dumped their dictator, as did many South American countries; liberation from the outside would not have succeeded.

The exceptions are nations that have already enjoyed personal freedom, before an authoritarian government took over. One of these rare cases was Nazi-Germany, whose citizens had tasted democracy during the Weimar Republic. Don't try that with Iran, though, whose fundamentalist theocracy is as little loved by many as the Taliban were in Afghanistan. Interference by strangers will only result in Iranians closing ranks against the intruders.

MANNERS

In all important aspects, my two favorite countries are truly free. In Germany as well as in the United States, you can vote in fair elections, speak your mind and may do pretty much as you please, as long as it is within the law. It is in much less crucial, little but potentially annoying details where they differ, and where stereotypes have it wrong as so often.

Whenever I felt the need to ask for permission to smoke, a former American boss of mine (coincidentally, a Dutchman by birth) used to reply, "It's a free country", while on the other hand I have frequently heard and read that in Germany "*Alles ist verboten*". A closer look and hands-on experience in both countries, however, tell a different story.

Go hiking in any California State or Regional Park (without your dog of course, as that is *verboten* even on a leash), but don't look forward to a cold beer from your car's cooler at the end of the trail (or, heaven forbid, even a cigarette, if you are the filthy kind) – alcohol and smoking are *verboten*. In the state of Indiana, don't try to buy alcohol on a Sunday or to carry your toddler through the bar to the outdoor patio for a family lunch, that is *verboten*. And if you think your strong teenage son can help you carry a case of beer from the supermarket to your car in the parking lot, you'll soon find out that that is *verboten*, too.

Any citizen of the *"Alles verboten"* country will shake his/her head in amazement or disbelief, as they are used to taking their dog even into the next restaurant after a hike (usually *verboten* here). And if that hike took them along a lakeshore or across a pasture to a mountain top, that trail was open to the public even when crossing private property – as opposed to the familiar "No Trespassing" signs here.

So does Germany have a greater teenage drinking problem than the US? Do you see brawls between drunken adults in public parks? Are beaches and nature preserves littered with cigarette butts? In fact, none of the above, although nothing is *verboten.* How come?

The answer may lie in the other little freedoms Americans are used to taking, such as leaving cigarette butts behind wherever they smoke, although an ashtray might only be a few feet away, or empty cans and candy wrappers even along nature trails. "Clean up after your pet" and "Pack it in, pack it out" are as closely adhered to as the "Do not litter" signs along highways, where cleaning crews must collect garbage at regular intervals. In the Old Country, not leaving a mess behind under your theater or ball park seat is considered part of basic manners, like not putting your feet on the chair across from you or yawning into somebody's face without covering your mouth. Parents, by the way, pay attention to these matters and don't see teaching fundamental behavior as part of the schools' educational responsibility.

Manners here largely consist of not speaking impolitely into somebody's face, but according to Kathy Griffin only behind people's back. You decide which of the small freedoms are nicer to have...

Marriage

Just in case you by now have categorized me as a left-wing radical disrespectful of all venerable institutions (such as POTUS, Congress, democracy and – just read on – patriotism, to name a few), here is an example for me upholding traditional values: I firmly believe marriage should be reserved for the union between man and woman. Not for religious reasons (You may by now already have your doubts about my religiosity), but for biological ones.

Even traditional marriage is open to various interpretations in different parts of the world. In Italy, supporting a mistress on the side is acceptable, as long as you don't neglect your family. In France and in (very catholic) Greece grieving mistresses have stood side-by-side with the widow at a celebrity's grave, and nobody seemed to be shocked. In Islamic countries on the other hand, less than faithful spouses can legally be stoned to death (Women only, of course, since men are entitled to multiple wives up to the size of a harem). The US are somewhere in between: Polygamy is still practiced and largely tolerated in certain states, but legal only if sequential. So if you want to marry husband number four or eight, make sure you have divorced his predecessors first.

Still, marriages are meant to be for life here and in Germany, although 50% end in divorce sooner or later. So we keep our fingers crossed for our son and his lovely wife, and the chances are good. I have been married to the same wife for close to 40 years by now, and our son's in-laws are not far behind. The secret? Don't get married at the first crush (Crushes are great, but don't last, and Viagra is not a permanent solution either), but wait for somebody complementary in important areas and compatible in the others. Any marriage will still have it ups and downs, but it is a lot easier to stick it out, if the conditions up front were right. Staying together is definitely worth it, when the result is a relationship of trust and mutual respect, with a whiff of good business, i.e. shared responsibilities. Enduring love bears more similarity to a good friendship than to a passionate crush, and does indeed last for a lifetime. I have an old (in every sense of the word) Bavarian friend, who told his wife that while he could not promise that he would never fall for a one-night stand, he could guarantee her that he would never, ever leave her for anybody in the world.

That declaration may not be compatible with any standard bigot definition of marriage, but pretty well sums up what a good one is all about.

Mens Sana

Mens sana in corpore sano (a healthy mind in a healthy body), is what humans should strive for in life according to the Roman poet Juvenal. This advice is as good and valid today as it was then, but all too often not heeded.

60% of Americans are overweight (with a significant portion clinically obese), and Germans are trying hard to catch up. Even the traditionally slim Japanese are beginning to develop a weight problem, and Latinos are gaining too much not only in the US. The accompanying health problems already result in a 6 years shorter life expectancy of obese people, not much better than that of smokers (8 years shorter than average). The main causes of this worrisome trend, experts agree, are unhealthy diet (too much of the wrong food) and an increasingly sedentary life style – couch potato being the technical term. Both are factors that could be fairly easily controlled: Eat less and what is known to be good for you, and work out in your spare time. Instead, fast food restaurants continue to advertise their steadily growing super-size portions, and apparel manufacturers quietly increase the size of their garments. My wife used to wear size 6, when we moved here more than 30 years ago. Now she needs size 4 or even 2 – and she did not shrink. Still you see many grossly overweighed women squeeze themselves into pants that obviously are too small, probably since they don't want to face reality and move up in size, while men solve the problem by letting the blubber hang over the belt.

On the other hand, especially if you are fortunate enough to live in the Sun Belt, you will find the group of health enthusiasts well represented – not just surfer dudes, but professionals and homemakers independent of gender and age, who are taking care of their body. They lead an active life, work out, jog or power walk, and show off their trim figure with pride. With them, however, one often cannot help but notice that the other part of the recommendation suffers from neglect. While they can tell you which fatty acid to avoid and which vegetable juice is best for you, they are at a loss, when the conversation moves on to art, science or politics. They don't regularly attend concerts, visit museums or read good books, but unlike their bodies leave their minds severely undernourished with the exception of occasional junk food.

So it continues to be a rare pleasure, when you find a healthy-looking person, who has spent as much time, effort and money on caring for his or her mind as for their body, and with whom you can discuss in a meaningful way topics that matter to both of you. Juvenal would agree – in the long run, the best maintained body is not very attractive, if it houses an anorexic mind.

NEWS

Residents and citizens of both my favorite countries can enjoy the not always fully appreciated privilege of having access to uncensored news from all over the world, as long as the free media consider an event newsworthy and of interest to their viewers, listeners or readers (and in most cases, their advertisers). In this latter restriction unfortunately lies a major catch, since the ultimate selection of items is based on the media's decision.

There is for instance in the US a 24 hour news channel on TV (the "Need to Know Network") that has made up your, the viewer's, mind for you. In addition to countless commercials, you need to know hours of celebrity gossip (aka "Entertainment News"), prejudiced judgments on heinous crimes (the gorier the better) or similarly valuable information, but certainly not about elections in Denmark (where??) or a natural disaster in New Zealand, unless at least a few thousand people perish. If you really care about such details, you have to be lucky enough to have access to BBC (Thank heaven for the Commonwealth), the Deutsche Welle, if your local university channel bothers to transmit it every day (Thank you, ITV) or PBS, which for its objective broadcasting is under regular attack by viewers not like you and me (who support it).

As an alternative, there are of course the traditional printed media – newspapers, if you can and are willing to take the daily time to read them and have made up your mind about your preferred spin, and weeklies, if not. The problem here is the same as above: In the US, you can read pages about the latest scandals involving a congressman (There are always some) or in Germany about corporate misdoings (same), but if you are interested in other topics (Did you know they have elections in Norway and environmental problems in Tonga?), you better subscribe to "The Economist" – British again – or at least to "The Week" (Bless you – American, but by subscription only). So freedom of the press is great and essential, but what it is used for in the free world is pretty abysmal. Do we get what we ask for, or do we only get what somebody thinks is good and enough for us? Here in the US the government (i.e. the FCC) has the answer: To avoid confusing us, it would be just fine to receive the same messages by your local newspaper and TV station, both owned by the same conglomerate.

So while we theoretically have unlimited access to untainted and uncensored news, to hear or read the whole story we have to take refuge to the Internet, which – living in either of my favorite countries – is readily available. If you don't have or do not use this source, however, you are stuck with what the media think you need to know - and they seem to hold you and me in rather low esteem.

OLYMPIANS

No doubt sports have been commercialized to an often nauseating extent. Successful athletes are celebrities and treated and paid like rock stars, sponsored with mind-boggling amounts of money, traded like other high-value merchandise, and still prostitute themselves in TV commercials for just about any company that pays well. Universally condemned but widespread doping is just a side effect of this situation, as average athletes try to move into the ranks of superstars and their corresponding income.

If you watched the opening ceremony of any recent summer Olympiad, you might have felt confirmed that it is indeed all about business, Beijing just being the most recent culmination. Hollywood could not have produced a better show, and Baron de Coubertin would have cringed at the thought what became of his revival of the antique original.

All this does not matter, however, when you watch the actual competitions. Young (and sometimes even not so young) men and women, who have worked hard for years and often decades to improve their performance, give their honest best, often reaching higher than ever before. Occasional faux-pas not withstanding (faux-pas is French, as are certain swimmers), true sportsmanship prevails, and it is heart-warming to see fierce competitors congratulate each other on their accomplishments or embrace in a consoling hug after a serious mishap. Almost more important is to see the spectators who, while of course rooting for the home team, almost equally enthusiastically applaud victorious visitors. Many small and occasional grand gestures indicate that internal team spirit and camaraderie across national lines are well-off and that fairness usually continues beyond the venue gates.

So while the Olympic show will undoubtedly go on, M. de Coubertin can continue to rest in peace after all. The Olympic Games still serve their original purpose because of the Olympians' admirable spirit and dedication, and audiences who appreciate it.

PAIN AND GAIN

"No pain, no gain" is a rule that has largely not applied to our postwar generation in Europe and in the US. During WW II, Americans made a tremendous effort to overcome the Axis war machine and richly deserved the following decades, when many were finally able to fulfill the "American Dream" of having a family, owning their house and car and work and live in peace. On the other side of the Atlantic, Germans worked hard to rebuild their country from rubble and ashes thus creating the "*Wirtschaftswunder*" (economic miracle), with the eventual generous help of their victorious former enemies (Marshall Plan and Berlin Airlift after Versailles and Morgenthau).

Our generation and the following ones have enjoyed the fruit of these efforts without giving it much thought. The pursuit of happiness and prosperity are seen as an entitlement and taken for granted; immediate gratification is expected. Only recently have people realized that times are changing, and it remains to be seen how well we will be able to handle serious challenges we were confronted with never before.

Germany has built an all but complete social net protecting its citizens against any undeserved hardships (and a few deserved ones) without paying enough attention to its consequences for the country's finances and competitiveness. To correct the situation, working hours are being increased, benefits reduced and taxes raised. Still, the state cannot guarantee the next generation the degree of protection we have gotten accustomed to, and individuals will have to shoulder greater responsibility to provide for their old age.

The situation is worse in the United States, where spending at all levels has been more reckless, the lifestyle of many more wasteful, and the high standard of living often based on credit rather than assets. The adjustment will therefore have to be even more dramatic, if the goal is to have debt-free families live responsibly in a country not largely owned by other nations.

While Germans seem to have accepted reality (albeit somewhat grudgingly), there until recently was an American presidential candidate promising to continue the prohibitively expensive Iraq war until final victory, while balancing the budget without raising taxes. (Contrary to malicious rumors, he did not claim also to be able to turn water into wine after walking on it first.) His applauding audience would probably also have loved the final tunes played by the board band of the "Titanic".

Gain without pain? Keep on dreaming…

Patriotic Pride

Pride is best reserved for own accomplishments, or for contributions to those of others. As a resident of the U.S. of A., I could be proud of any achievements during my stay in this country, or – stretching it a bit – maybe even of the fact that many years ago, I was deemed worthy enough to be accepted as a permanent resident by the merciless guardian of such things, the INS. I cannot possibly, however, be proud of the Founding Fathers or the hard labor of many subsequent generations of citizens and immigrants, the result of which I am now enjoying.

Nagged by jealousy I therefore ask myself why so many Americans are full of pride. Have they all contributed significantly to their country's greatness to develop this feeling, or is it enough to have been lucky enough to have been born here (rather than for instance in Mongolia or Congo) for justification? Does selling a consumer product assembled in Mexico from parts produced in China provide sufficient satisfaction, or does it take slapping the label "Produced with pride in America" on a box of something?

So I continue to be overwhelmed by the ubiquitous presence of symbols of patriotic pride, from the huge image of the star-spangled banner on the dry cleaner's plastic cover of my pants ("The colors that don't run" – I hope he is right) to the real thing hanging limp on a portable pole, while its proud owner shoots up beer cans in the desert. Is everybody flying the flag a good steward of the land, a staunch defender of its values, a committed builder of its moral and economic strength? As a humble resident awed by so much achievement, I must accept the fact that I may never be able to match the standard for citizenship, and resign myself to be fortunate enough to be a resident, bogged down by my antiquated requirements for the development of personal pride.

Which is probably just as well, since there is only a thin line separating patriotism from arrogance and aggression. Parades and military ceremonies in dress uniforms are one thing, preemptive wars another, and unwavering leadership ("staying the course") does not necessarily guarantee the right direction. So while it must feel good to have a passport requesting all whom it may concern to permit the bearer "to pass without delay or hindrance and in case of need to give all lawful aid and protection" (my European one states laconically, "This passport is the property of the Federal Republic of Germany"), I feel safer traveling with mine in many parts of the world than our American friends with theirs. Maybe I should have a bit of patriotic pride after all...

Peer Pressure

We only learned about peer pressure after moving to the U.S., but since it seems to affect mainly young people, I do not know whether it is a local disease or a worldwide generational phenomenon. Among students, its positive effect unless taken to extremes is the increased ambition to excel in academic subjects and sports. Often, however, its negative aspect prevails and stimulates even young teenagers to enter the Keeping-Up-with-the-Jones world.

You simply HAVE to wear the latest fashion shirt and sneakers, preferably adorned with a celebrity logo demonstrating its priciness. You HAVE to own the fanciest cell phone to be able to take pictures, text and navigate, and you definitely must show a long list of "friends" on one of the social network websites as proof of your popularity. Kids have killed for running shoes and mobile phones, and committed suicide after receiving hate mail on the Internet.

It is difficult to understand this urge to follow and imitate trendsetters, as opposed to standing out from the crowd. Is it lack of self-confidence that experience and success later in life may cure? Or is it the reflection of the widespread absence of an independent personal value system that should have been instilled through education and example-setting?

We always called our son by the first of his two given names, rather uncommon and somewhat old-fashioned here. Once a teenager, he only wanted to be known by his middle name, the most frequent in his generation in America. Maybe he feels safer, when it is called and a dozen young men raise their hands.

Personal Limitations

Many people seem to have a hard time recognizing and accepting the limits of their education and intelligence. Nobody has a problem acknowledging the physical superiority of sport celebrities, but when it comes to brain capacity, even average minds feel at par with the preeminent representatives of science, and entitled to denounce sophisticated theories and whole fields of research the names of which they can barely spell.

I would love to know and understand more about astronomy and physics (too abstract and mathematical for me) and even down-to-earth disciplines like geology and paleontology (I prefer living organisms), but have to admit that I probably never will – unless a specialist with patience and good teaching skills takes the time to help me on specific topics. As a consequence I in many areas have to rely on the judgment of greater and more educated minds, and have resigned to live with strings, black energy and a big bang without really comprehending such esoteric matters.

So I am always amazed when I hear talk show hosts on national television generously spread their profound wisdom on anything from the economy to global warming and evolution to the purpose of humanity, without as much as blinking. Considering how moronic their drivel is in my field of expertise, I can only guess about the validity of their gospel in areas I am not familiar with. What really makes me shudder, however, is how many viewers might take those unqualified comments as the truth (since of course TV or radio stations otherwise would not pay outrageous sums of money to attract these motor mouths) and incorporate them into their own opinions.

As a result, you find the most opinionated and intolerant fellow human beings often to be amongst the least educated. But even partially educated ones often have the tendency to ignore their limitations and feel qualified to venture into fields they know little about, but offer ultimate verdicts with mind-boggling authority. For instance we have in San Diego a TV "meteorologist", who has a hard time predicting tomorrow's weather (in a part of the world known for its constant climate) but does not hesitate to take on the hundreds of the world's most knowledgeable specialists on global warming. It goes without saying that this person has a stage for his ludicrous ideas on the TV station's website and gets invited by right-wing talk show hosts to further spread his revelations. Not funny, if you keep in mind that even listeners aware of their limitations might take nonsense seriously, if it is presented in a forum believed to be credible.

In our free world anybody can publish just about anything, and it is up to the individual to apply moderation based on his/her realization of their own competence. And while modesty and outright humbleness are wide-spread virtues amongst great thinkers, noisy publicity-seekers hardly ever display these characteristics.

Physical Pain

Americans are the leading consumers of painkillers in the world. Whatever hurts or just bothers you – you pop a pill, and you are ready to play tennis, ski, chase your grandchild around or work in the construction business; just watch the TV commercials. And why not? What is the purpose of pain other than to annoy or even torture you? (I am not talking about severe chronic pain such as associated with migraine, certain cancers, rheumatoid arthritis and other serious diseases, but about your occasional headache, sprained ankle, shoulder or knee after exercise, that sort of thing – this is where the market for big Pharma and their OTC painkillers is.)

Pain is a signal your body has evolved to send you as an alert: Something is wrong, look for the cause, take care of it before it gets worse. Painkillers extinguish the signal, but don't cure the problem, which may become much more serious if ignored. If you feel stabbed in the back, avoid heavy lifting or change your posture if you have to do it, don't just grab the medicine bottle. If you are sore after a long hike or an afternoon in the gym, live with it and watch it lessen after more exercise: It's a good monitor of your progress. And if it does not get less or even increases, listen to your body and jog on a trail in the woods rather than on pavement. Mother Nature has developed this alarm system over many millennia, and you would be well advised to respond to it rather than mute and ignore it. When your time comes, your brain will shut off all warning signals, and the moments before death will be painless – you don't have to practice now.

Mental pain such as bouts of depression are often handled the same way. Just talk to your doctor, and he/she will gladly give you a prescription. Whether you can't sleep or your child is hyperactive, there is nothing that cannot be remedied without bothering to find out why.

PIONEER SPIRIT

Think of the early settlers, who came from established Europe to strike out on their own in an unknown and often hostile country, with sometimes extreme climate, difficult terrain and unfamiliar vegetation and wildlife. There was nobody to turn to except their neighbor struggling with similar problems, and it was up to them and their tenacity and ingenuity to succeed or perish.

Coming from densely populated and heavily regulated Germany, I was looking forward to encounter this pioneer spirit of people used to be self-sufficient and carefully guarding their individual freedom against a mushrooming federal bureaucracy (The latter was an assumption, as all bureaucracies tend to mushroom). Was I in for a surprise.

First of all I expected the great outdoors to infiltrate American life – this is how the country started (a few settlers in the wilderness), and sure there would be a continuing intimate relationship with nature. There came the first epiphany: At least the city-dwelling Americans (We started out and have always lived in or near cities) were actually afraid of the outdoors and avoided it whenever possible. No beer gardens or outdoor dining, as there could be dreaded bugs, but air-conditioned or overheated restaurants (where you needed a sweater in the summer and were comfortable in short sleeves in the winter). Fruit, vegetables and mushrooms were only safe to eat when purchased in a supermarket and preferably bland

– no competition, when we hunted delicious wild mushrooms in Midwestern forests. I still remember us picking gorgeous pears in an abandoned orchard, when a passer-by asked us, "Can you eat these?". In the great (no longer Wild) West, where we live now, we were delighted to see a real coyote or a real bobcat on our property; a friend's first question was, "Did you call Animal Control?"

Secondly, I assumed pioneers would learn from their mistakes and get better at avoiding them in the future. Wrong again – today's free spirits find somebody else to blame, sue or threaten to, and settle out of court for undisclosed amounts of money.

And finally, in another embodiment of the pioneer spirit, there are the big corporations as a result of successful entrepreneurs. They have preserved their independence, unfettered from undue government interference and self-regulate in a free market – until they run into trouble because of mismanagement or frivolous risk-taking. Then all of a sudden they clamor for the government to their rescue, whether they are banks, car manufacturers or other poor victims of deplorable circumstances.

There are signs of a return to earlier values in some areas: patio dining is in, people pay extra for organically grown vegetables in the local farmers market, and I have been able to eat in a restaurant in the summer without putting on a sweatshirt. So keep it up, America: Let the dummies pay for their mistakes (Trust me, I have made mine and paid for them), and let companies mismanaged by grossly overpaid executives go under, as any small entrepreneur would.

It is still time to reinstall what made America great: unlimited opportunities to succeed, if you are good, and to go down in flames, if you are not.

POLITICS

Politics are different between Europe and the United States. Not that politicians are – most of them are equally untruthful all over the world and will say anything to get elected or when caught in an ambiguous situation. What differs is people's attitude towards them.

Europeans have long accepted the sad reality and take campaign promises with a large lump of salt. They are also used to seeing politicians involved in a scandal continue to lie, until the damaging evidence becomes overwhelming. As a consequence, declarations by government representatives frequently meet with skepticism, cases of deception revealed with cynicism ("What else did you expect?").

Americans on the other hand tend to naively believe their elected officials, although they must know by now that have been lied to profusely - by their outgoing Republican president and his staff as well as by his Democratic predecessor. Many citizens of this country react with disbelief or genuine indignation, when they discover that their government has been less than forthright with embarrassing facts. They have not quite accepted that politicians everywhere spin the truth, pander to powerful special interests and cover up what they don't want the public to know. Some can do this with such a straight face that I am wondering, whether they themselves actually believe what they are saying.

There was this presidential candidate for example, who bragged about having contributed to making the country prosperous, while the economy is on the brink of recession with almost daily more bad news (Maybe he was talking about the rich who make more than $5 million a year and don't know how many houses they own…). He also boasted of having fought the big oil companies, who reap billions of dollars in profit off the until recently record-high gas prices at the pump, and having taken on Big Pharma, whose drugs are more expensive here than in our neighboring countries. At least his claim about having fought corruption in both parties seems justified, as members of congress now see forced to hide their ill-gotten gains in freezer boxes.

Fortunately there was also an alternative to politics as usual – a candidate stating clearly and unfazed by criticism what he stands for. No drilling for oil off the American coast, as it just does not make sense (But then, maybe a little bit of drilling, just to help out), and an end to America's unpopular and hugely expensive war in Iraq within a year (Or maybe 16 months, if the military agrees, of course). Is the strong wind of change already turning into not much more than a gentle breeze? Which would of course still be better than the lull promised by the other guy.

As a result of the realization that American politicians are no better than those elsewhere, I have recently heard people say in frustration that they won't vote at all. That is of course the wrong conclusion and highly irresponsible. Even if you can only choose the lesser of several evils, you owe it to your country and the world to do so – and during the last election, fortunately most Americans did.

Religion

Religions have always been and continue to be a major driving force in the history of humankind, which unfortunately also includes the cause of countless conflicts and cruel wars. Whether it is Ireland or the Balkans, the Near or the Far East – Catholics and Protestants, Christians and Jews, Muslims and Hindus often felt the best way to spread their belief was by killing the infidels, and some still do.

This would be easy to comprehend in primitive cultures worshiping many gods (one for each natural phenomenon they don't understand) and disputing whether Zeus, Jupiter or Wotan reigns supreme. It eludes me, however, how educated people in the twenty-first century assume their one omniscient and omnipotent god would be petty enough to punish human beings striving to live a decent life, but are following the "wrong" middle-management.

Does tolerance have to be limited to agnostics, who accept that they don't know which belief is the "right" one? Who realize that some 12 billion years ago (not 4,000, please) something happened none of us can truly understand – whether it was caused by an impersonal "law of nature" (whatever that term actually means) or a personalized eternal being, who presumably could not care less whether you wear a head scarf or work Saturdays.

For most of us it is difficult to see our individual existence as the consequence of a random event with no inherent purpose as M. Sartre claims, but we much prefer believing in a deeper meaning ("opium for the people" according to Karl Marx). But why on earth does that have to involve proselytizing, torturing and murdering others for adhering to a different version of the same basic belief? How about applying all that passion instead to protecting this great planet the creator has entrusted us with? Perhaps the Live-and-let-live attitude of a relaxed faithful looks more acceptable from above than that of a better-than-thou bigot.

Come judgment day, this might actually count more in your favor than having converted or extinguished a seemingly lost soul.

Right to Life

This is a term that in this country is firmly associated with human embryos or even fertilized eggs and their plea for survival, and the topic of endless heated discussions between passionate defenders and equally committed pro choice activists. Nobody likes abortions – they are traumatic for the mother and deadly for the offspring, and should only be a very last resort, if everything else has failed. "Everything else" primarily means contraception, which is of course shunned by the extreme Right, the Catholic Church and, yes, this country's outgoing president, who thinks celibacy is the cure for not just Africa's problems. If you are pregnant after – Heaven forbid – premarital sex, incest or rape, or if bearing and giving birth to a child could kill you, tough luck for you.

Much less public attention is focused on an at least to me more disturbing phenomenon, the spreading disrespect for human life, once it has left the womb. Teenagers kill others for the latest electronic gizmo or fashion accessory, muggers execute their victims even after they surrendered their valuables. Robbers murder lowly sales clerks and customers just to silence eye witnesses, homeless and immigrants are beaten to death for no obvious reason, and frustrated students or disgruntled employees go on a killing spree before taking their own life. Of course all these are isolated events just as newborns thrown into dumpsters, but their frequency must be disconcerting to anybody holding life sacred.

Whether the cause is the ubiquitous violence and gore in movies, computer games and TV shows, or the lack of education by parents and institutions of learning may be subject to discussion (I think both contribute), but the scary fact remains: Human life is not considered worth much by an increasing number of our fellow human beings, here as well as in Europe. So don't talk to me about the right to life for embryos, as long as it is perfectly ok to have children watch decapitations by chainsaw on family TV, and guns are present in most households as America's favorite problem solvers.

The lack of respect for life is not limited to human interactions, by the way. It equally extends to other life forms, many of which took tens of thousands or even millions of years to evolve (or if you prefer, were created four thousand years ago by an Intelligent Designer). Whether it is a little freshwater fish and its only home in the way of a huge surface mine in Appalachia or an endangered plant obstructing a new development in California – who cares. Fascinatingly, many ardent right-to-lifers and other religious fundamentalists, who by definition should be staunch defenders of threatened living things, have no problem killing off other species to maximize profits instead of being good stewards of their God's creations.

As popular German wisdom knows, however, a fish stinks from his head. If a country has a president claiming God as his consultant, but eager to rape, pilfer and destroy his own homeland for the sake of short-term profit, what can you expect from his loyal followers? Maybe they want to see future generations colonize Mars, as said president envisions – after he has done all he could to make our planet uninhabitable? He probably does not care, since (if he is as religious as he claims to be) he already knows where he is going, with the blood of thousands of innocent victims on his hands. But does anybody really want to accompany him?

The alternative seems a lot more attractive. Respect life in all of its forms – from the tiny plant and little bug that are the result of countless generations of struggle to finally find their modest place, to the millions of disenfranchised and suffering humans all over the world. Do that, and then I'll join your fight for the right to life of fertilized eggs in a Petri dish.

Rocking the Boat

I have seen it over and over again in my field of science, but have heard that it is just as common in other areas from economy to politics to religion: If you question a generally accepted dogma, you are asking for major trouble. That was true in the past from Galileo to Wegener, and still holds true today. Whether you propose an earth-shaking new theory or report a minor finding not consistent with the establishment's prejudice, you will be faced with disbelief, contempt or outright animosity, dependant on the importance of your report and the personalities of the reigning specialists. If you are lucky, you will just be dismissed as a crackpot, but don't be surprised about vitriolic Letters to the Editor or personal hate mail. The response will be especially strident, if your discovery suggests an oversight or negligence on the side of the complacent opinion leaders, who could (should) have noticed your point much earlier, had they paid more attention. (This is the familiar NIH effect – Not invented here, so it can't be any good.)

At least in science you have the consolation that eventually the truth will prevail. As independent investigators publish similar observations and collect more data supporting your findings, the establishment (aka scientific community) will at some point grudgingly admit that you may actually have been right. Don't hold your breath, though, as this process may take years or even decades. In fields not accessible to rigorous testing, a growing group of supporting believers and/or historians may sooner or (more likely) later elevate your proposal to a level at par with the dominant and equally untestable assumption.

So think twice before you decide to expose yourself to the treatment reserved for heretics in all areas, rather than just rowing along with the majority. Don't forget, however, that sometimes it is necessary to rock the boat to get it moving. When you are stuck on an obstacle or in morass, all the rowing in the world won't result in progress.

Scientist-in-Chief

While the United States constitution bestows the title and function of "Commander-in-Chief" on the president, only recently has he also become the Scientist-in-Chief. As a consequence, he does not need a scientific advisory board, but due to his supreme education and resulting omniscience decides on his own what is scientific truth and how (if at all) it should be applied. Citizens of lesser intellect and education (including professional scientists) can then learn from The Decider and direct their research accordingly. Hot topics thus settled were for instance Global Warming/Climate Change (a myth requiring further study, but no action), Stem Cell Research (immoral and not to be funded) and Evolution (a hypothesis at par with Creationism/Intelligent Design).

This recent development of course represents major progress over the limited capabilities of the country's Founding Fathers. Sure, many of them were studied scholars in philosophy, science or liberal arts – but all were restricted to certain areas of expertise and accepted that deficiency. Even the successful businessmen amongst them had limited experience – none ever bankrupted an oil company. At least they publicly displayed their imperfections by speaking conventional English (Had there been an opportunity, they would probably have blandly said "nuclear"" instead of "nucular"), they walked rather than strutted and talked humbly instead of condescendingly.

Chances are though that future presidents will see their role again closer to what the founders of this great nation had in mind. Such focus might allow them actually to take care of the country's and its citizens' needs. Wouldn't that be a pleasant change?

SEX

A collection of thoughts on miscellaneous topics inevitably has to include sex, one of the most pleasant and indispensable human activities – not only human, since unless you are able to multiply by budding, runners or parthenogenesis, any living thing will sooner or later practice it. Human attitude towards it, however, varies greatly, with substantial differences between my two favorite countries and over time.

Europeans in general and Germans in particular see things quite relaxed. This starts at the toddler stage – two-year-olds of either gender are not considered sex objects and are allowed to run around freely and quite naked in public, from community pools to beer gardens to residential neighborhoods. So we were amazed (and admittedly amused), when we were told by concerned neighbors in Chicago land to dress our baby son at least in diapers, not to embarrass (or confuse?) their same-age daughter, who was wearing what looked like a Christmas ribbon for a bikini top. (I then remembered having seen photographs of Midwestern cows in the fifties wearing bras around their udders, and acknowledged the need to comply with community standards.)

The differences continue for teenagers, who in sexual matters are considered adults past 16 in Germany, past 18 here. If educated properly (primarily by the parents, but also through real sex education at school), a 17 year-old adolescent is mature enough to make decisions just as rationally as a 19 year-old.

Even adults in many European countries have a very different attitude towards sex from that of most Americans. Nudity is considered to be natural rather than obscene, and topless sunbathing is as common in Munich city parks as on a French beach. Nudism is an acceptable albeit not very widespread lifestyle, and an exposed female nipple on public television does not trigger a nationwide uproar (nor a fine for the TV station). Both genders sweat together in the nude in saunas and are mildly amused by American tourists entering in bathing suits. This does not reflect a sad deterioration of morals, but simply a more open view of what is natural. I much prefer if youngsters catch an occasional glimpse of a female breast over the daily exposure to the violence routinely displayed by oh-so family-friendly American television stations.

But then I am of course myself one of these lewd Europeans. I think for instance that the world's oldest profession should be legalized everywhere (just as soft drugs, by the way). By brushing prostitution under the carpet or outright criminalizing it, you don't prevent it. It is as common here as in Europe, but there it is regulated, here criminalized. From streetwalkers to escort services to massage parlors, you can find working girls anywhere in America, if you care to look for them. It is a lot safer for all involved though to patronize a registered professional in a German Eros Center or a Swiss hotel, when you know the women have their weekly health check-ups and you don't need to worry about abusive pimps, forced prostitution and organized crime. Remember what prohibition did for the Mafia? Many of today's bad guys would be out of business, if prostitution and recreational drugs would be legal.

I have more than once been asked by German friends, whether Americans only have sex in the dark and solely to procreate. I am in no position to answer that question, but certainly the sexual revolution of the sixties has been replaced with a holier-than-thou prudery by a very vocal part of the population. Sex is one of the greatest and least expensive pleasures available to anybody and deserves to be enjoyed responsibly. By declaring celibacy the most important human virtue, it is grossly overvalued though and assigned undue importance. While an extramarital fling does not speak for the self-control or the intelligence of a candidate for the country's highest office, we have had to endure much dumber presidents (whose preaching about celibacy for Africans and teenagers did not make them look any smarter).

So while not all Americans are violent prudes and not all Europeans filthy woosies, there is a statistically significant difference in attitude between the two continents. The father of a good local friend of ours founded – tongue in cheek – a "Church of the Cheerful Sinners" as a bridge; many Europeans would flock to it.

Sexual Harassment

Sexual harassment was a serious problem that had to be dealt with: Superiors abusing their standing to demand sexual favors from lowly workers, individuals being wronged or persecuted because of their different sexual orientation, employees being embarrassed by persistent obscene remarks by their colleagues.

Then, however, came political correctness to the U.S., and the pendulum swung to the extreme other side. I have been reprimanded for complimenting a female coworker on her new hairdo or her new dress (Both were deemed unprofessional remarks inappropriate in the workplace); my German secretary would have felt insulted had I not noted the change. I worked for a company that did not allow closed-door one-on-one meetings with a member of the other sex – kind of difficult, if you happen to be a male VP needing to discuss confidential salary issues with the female Director of Human Resources. (Fortunately she was of Greek origin and closed the door, while her secretary – American, but with a European sense of humor - loudly complained, "They are at it again".) Another, similarly concerned employer of mine had a dress code requiring women always to keep their shoulders covered even during muggy Midwestern summer days. (That changed, after a bold female manager of Israeli origin came to work in an evening gown covering her shoulders, but with a back cleavage all the way down to her very attractive butt.)

At the same time, we did not have similar rules and regulations in Germany. Admittedly, once in many years I had an underperforming (but generously blessed by Mother Nature) female employee showing up in my office in a see-through blouse and no bra. I told her to go home, get dressed and report back to work – no lasting damage done, but I could have felt quite harassed (although more commonly harassment happens the other way round).

In general, working relations in the Old Country were usually fine without many pages of Corporate Policy telling you what not to do. You could open a door for a female coworker without her feeling harassed and even help her into her coat or with her carry-on, rather than slam the door in her face and watch her struggle with her luggage. Could it be that European women are actually more emancipated than their American sisters, without completely abandoning their femininity?

There is light at the end of the tunnel, though. Recently I have encountered female professionals even here who don't feel threatened by a polite male colleague, and who have actually tolerated (enjoyed?) an occasional compliment. Maybe the pendulum is swinging again...

Small-town America

Like 80% of Americans, we have always lived in or close to cities, usually in suburbs or near-by bedroom communities. Small towns, however, have never stopped to impress us with their special charm: friendly unhurried inhabitants, safe neighborhoods, no traffic jams – a reflection of what much of the country might have looked like in the early fifties. In fact, we recently came back from a short vacation in just one of these towns in southern New Mexico and loved it. Everything you needed for a content life was available at reasonable cost, and if you felt the urge to spend a fortune on fancy wardrobe and accessories (as some small-town mayors might), the next big city was within a day's driving reach. Based on the average family income in this town as published by the local Chamber of Commerce, however, most of its inhabitants were probably not in a position to follow that urge, and did not seem to mind.

If I compare this life-style with that of the rich and famous or the rightly much maligned greed-is-good Wallstreet types (not limited to Wallstreet), who after raking in millions now complain that they are loosing the shirt on their back, I know where I would much rather live and fit in without a problem.

Would I then also want to see the mightiest country in the world run by a president with a lovable small-town mentality? Definitely not. This job requires a profound understanding of the majority of the country, from big city ghettos to affluent gated communities in addition to rural settings, the experience of having traveled to foreign countries to understand their way of thinking, and preferably a multicultural background. Such a person would be qualified to be a good steward of this heterogeneous country as well as the respected leader of the free world.

A well-rounded personality meeting all these criteria is of course rare and hard to find. Hard, but as we now know, not impossible.

Socialism

Socialism is applied communism, which in its pure form (Marxism) demands equal wealth for all citizens and public ownership of all resources and production facilities. That this ideology does not work, since it is incompatible with the inherently ambitious human nature, has been proven by the not so distant history. Its extreme opposite, pure capitalism with its unbridled greed and no compassion for less fortunate members of the society is equally unacceptable to ordinary humans, who have not evolved to be solely egotistical, and has also failed, as has become obvious even more recently.

As so often, the truth lies somewhere in the middle. To motivate its members to fulfill their potential and reach or exceed high goals, society has to offer incentives and appropriate (not extravagant) rewards; a free market and limited taxation are essential components of such a system. Nations like Sweden have discovered the damage excessive taxes (more than 90% in the highest bracket) can cause and learnt from their mistake. On the other hand, no country expected to be called civilized should allow hundreds or thousands of millionaires and billionaires, while a significant fraction of its population lives in poverty and lacks even the fundamentals of a dignified life. As in a large corporation, in every society there cannot be only stellar performers, but the hard-working average at the basis needs to be able to participate in the common success.

During a few particularly successful years in my professional life I made several hundred thousand dollars, and while I like every reasonable person tried to minimize my tax burden, I always felt it was a good problem to have, since it reflected my high income. And yes, I thought it was my duty towards my host country to pay my share; the arrogant statement that only poor people pay taxes never struck me as particularly patriotic.

To call a president "Marxist" for striving to redistribute some of the huge corporate gains and massive individual incomes to the many not able to make a living in spite of their hard efforts shows at best an abysmal lack of comprehension of this term, and more likely the commentator's own greed and disregard for everybody else. "Marxist" FDR pulled this country out of a deep recession, and many of today's suddenly job- and homeless Americans would probably not mind having at least a guaranteed health insurance and decent unemployment benefits like Europeans living in a "socialist" country.

But then maybe the knowledge of the "Inauguration Package" offered by a ritzy Washington hotel (5 days of accommodation plus 2 tickets for the parade and ball and a small piece of designer jewelry for a paltry $50,000) will make them feel better.

STEM CELL RESEARCH

This is of course a loaded topic – loaded with emotions particularly on the side of those completely unencumbered by any scientific knowledge and understanding such as the Religious Right and the outgoing president. So let's start with the basics.

First of all, "Embryonic Stem Cells" are a bit of a misnomer, as they are usually not derived from embryos but their predecessors (morulas or blastulas), largely undifferentiated aggregations of cells. You have to be pretty extreme or outright fanatic to call such a lump of cells (which is frequently aborted naturally when trying to nest *in utero*) an embryo. Secondly, most embryonic stem cell lines are derived from the left-over of in vitro fertilizations, when sperm cells have fertilized egg cells in a Petri dish. Usually anywhere from 6 to 12 to more fertilized eggs are allowed to develop to the morula or blastula stage, since few of them (if any) will take after implantation into the mother's uterus. The remainder is frozen away in liquid nitrogen – to be used, if the first attempts fail, or to be discarded, if the parenting couple was lucky enough to have the number of offspring they desire. "Discarded" means killed in an autoclave by high temperature and pressure, then disposed of with other medical waste (used syringes, stool samples and the like). You have to be rather cold-hearted (or did I mention fanatical?) to claim that this is a better use than serving as the basis for medical research towards up to now untreatable diseases from Parkinson's to diabetes to blindness to spinal cord injuries.

An alternative to "embryonic" stem cells is adult stem cells, recoverable from blood and other tissues. The main difference is that "embryonic" stem cells are omnipotent (i.e. can develop into all tissues), while adult stem cells are pluripotent (can develop into some, but not all types of tissue). At present, the use of both is highly experimental, and both avenues need to be pursued to find one that works in real life, the treatment of patients. The objection voiced by some scientists is based on the potential for abuse: Embryos might be created specifically for research purposes, which indeed would be unethical. Self-imposed or mandated restraint of conscientious scientists, however, has never prevented the development of new technologies and their abuse. Otto Hahn and Fritz Strassmann did not mean to develop the atomic bomb, when they discovered nuclear fission, and the Asilomar Conference did not prevent cloned mammals (with much more to come).

The general discussion about ethics and moral relating to stem cell research, on the other hand, is strongly reminiscent of that about "pro choice" versus "right to life", and often conducted by the same groups with similar emotional arguments, although the situation is quite different. So please rethink your position. Who is more important, a lump of cells or a human being suffering from an incurable disease?

Whatever the result of your thoughts may be – try to understand the other side. It is not that difficult.

TERM LIMIT

There should not be a term limit for the president in a democracy. Reaching lofty goals or repairing major damage may require more than eight years, and if a president is competently on the right track with the support of the people, he should be allowed to continue, if reelected. If on the other hand he or she is not reelected or not even re-nominated by the party, this would send a much clearer signal than the present excuse of not being allowed to run again.

Where a term limit would be highly desirable is with members of Congress. That would take care of the Old Boys Club once and for all, and provide a strong incentive to Senators and Representatives actually to accomplish something during their eight years, other than circular discussions and mutual adulation. Their own wellbeing and pork barrel projects for their constituents might no longer be their top priority, but making lasting improvements for the country.

At least it is worth a try – the result could not be worse than what we have now.

THE AMERICAN DREAM

Dependent on who is dreaming, the American Dream can have quite different meanings. Most commonly it stands for the rise from poverty to prosperity, and while few dishwashers ended up as multimillionaires, countless immigrants (me included) found that hard work in this country usually is rewarded with a fairly carefree life sooner than elsewhere.

If you have an advanced degree in science or technology, the opportunities for a successful career in your field of expertise were (and still are in many areas) greater than in your home country – an important component of my own dream. When I left Germany in 1972 with a couple of trunks and duffle bags and no job, there was not even a curriculum for Molecular Biology at German universities. I had taken all sorts of classes various professors of biochemistry and biology had told me would probably be necessary or at least useful, and completed a Ph.D. thesis resulting in a degree in (officially not yet existing) Molecular Biology. Although my future American employers were a bit puzzled by the fact that I did not have a B.S. nor M.S. in my field (again not yet established in the Old Country), this was not a serious problem and totally acceptable at top universities and research institutions. Try this elsewhere, and you will quickly discover how cumbersome red tape can be.

Even more important and outright essential is another component of the American Dream for immigrants from oppressed countries Here they can live freely without fear of persecution, voice dissenting opinions and – if they become naturalized citizens – vote in fair elections. Even having moved from another democracy, I noticed a quantitative difference: Certain blunt criticisms of leading politicians could land you in court there (for insult or libel), but are protected by the first amendment here. (Of course here you might receive death threats instead, but that is a different story.)

So why do you hear complaints these days that the American Dream is no longer true? Mainly, I think, because of unreasonable expectations. The acceptance of years of hard work along the way to success has frequently been replaced with the desire for immediate gratification, which combined with the unfortunate American addiction to the almost limitless use of credit can and often does lead to disaster. We have had young neighbors with two low-paying jobs "owning" a house, car, RV, motorcycle and boat – "owning" meaning they could afford the minimum monthly payments for all of this. We have also met middle-aged families with several children and variable interest-only mortgages on their super-sized homes in expensive locations. What do you expect happens, when the main bread winner looses his/her job in an economic downturn?

I am convinced the American Dream is as alive and well as it has always been, but you have to work as hard and patiently for its fulfillment as you always had to. There is no country in the world offering more opportunities and greater freedom to use them than this one, imperfections (which this book admittedly dwells on) not-withstanding.

Always keep in mind – only in America can a person with limited intelligence and no proven track record become president and even get reelected. So Carpe diem.

THE AMERICAN WAY

Having been raised in an Old Country, we initially had a hard time understanding how Americans could afford their affluent lifestyle. Young couples not even half our age owned their home, two cars and the latest toys we could only dream of in our rented apartment. The solution to the riddle became clear, once we realized that "owning" means making just enough money to keep up with one's monthly payments.

Admittedly, we old-fashioned immigrants also share ownership of our house with the mortgage company, but we always bought cars or other big ticket items only when we thought we could afford to pay for them in full. The "No payment and no interest due until…" never enticed us to live beyond our means.

Eventually of course the unavoidable had to happen, and the house of cards came crashing down. The adjustable, interest only mortgage suddenly required exorbitant monthly payments, the new furniture surprisingly did end up costing money after all, and you can only borrow so much from your (401)k, if you have one. Reality shows on TV might be fun to watch, true reality unfortunately is not.

An underlying cause of the reckless borrowing and spending is the widespread demand for immediate gratification – take what you can get now and enjoy it today. The federal government has blazed the trail by amassing a huge amount of national debt, and by trying to rape and pillage the country as much as possible. Drill for oil while it lasts, mine, lumber and graze as long as there is something left, and leave it to future generations to enjoy the inheritance. I understand the plight of the Carolina fisherman who wants to continue over-harvesting horseshoe crabs for bait, or that of the rancher urging to kill off wolves, prairie dogs and everything else interfering with his traditional business of raising as much cattle as the range can feed, but it is not fundamentally different from that of the Silesian weaver threatened by the mechanical loom, the coal miner in the Ruhrgebiet relying on government subsidies, or the Japanese whaler systematically destroying the basis of his livelihood. Take what you can today, and let others worry about the future.

Another glaring and disturbing feature of the American Way is the evangelical zeal, with which its proponents attempt to spread it all over the world. For many, there are only two ways of life: the American and the wrong one. No matter what a country's history and culture might be – America's Jeffersonian democracy is the one size that is expected to fit all. Whenever Americans believe they have found something good (and it often actually is), they feel the irresistible urge to share it with everybody else, whether the recipient wants it or not. I am glad that about a quarter of Americans still smoke (albeit mostly in closets). Otherwise, any nation still allowing smoking in public places could be the next target for liberation.

Much can be said for the advantages of the American Way, and continuously is by this country's most fervent patriots. Having lived here half my life, I am still trying to distill what its additional key attributes might be, distinguishing it from the rest of the world in general, and my home country Germany in particular. What America lacks and needs most of all is the ability to learn from others' mistakes and successes, and emulate the latter. This is difficult (I as an individual have yet to master that skill), but there is hope. Not that long ago a leading news magazine published a series of articles on issues other nations seem to handle better, from healthcare to education, from Europe to Asia. And once America has found out that "staying the course" can also mean throwing good money after bad and kicking a dead horse, then the revelation that one cannot liberate a country against it's ruling minority's will (and that of the oppressed minority) will not come as a surprise (Does Vietnam ring a bell?). If Sunnis and Shiites want to be at each other's throat, then even the hundred–year-occupation considered by some is not going to change that.

Once Americans replace self-absorption and swagger with understanding and cooperation, and finger-pointing with constructive planning, this will be as great a country as some claim it to be already now – and the American Way will be generally accepted as most desirable.

THE DAY AFTER TOMORROW

German is a rather complicated and often long-winded and cumbersome language (Mark Twain had a bit to say about that in his "The Awful German Language"), and yet there is one simple word ("*übermorgen*") for "the day after tomorrow", while it takes four words to address that same day in English. Is this an insignificant linguistic detail, or does it reflect a profound difference in attitude towards the future? Do Germans think (and worry, remember "*Angst*"?) more about the future than Americans, who might live more for today and at most tomorrow, but are less concerned with "*übermorgen*", the day(s) after?

When the economy tanks and unemployment is high, Germans save and deepen the slump by not buying anything but the bare essentials. Americans on the other hand continue to shop even during doubtful times, thus keeping the economy humming full-blast, usually to the surprise of most analysts predicting a down-turn. Saving money for an uncertain future is not an issue – as long as you can come up with the minimum payment on your credit card and your monthly payments for your house, cars, boat etc. you are ok and can enjoy the immediate gratification for your toils and labor, according to the familiar rule "He who dies with the most toys wins". When then all of a sudden and unexpectedly (?) reality hits and debts become due or interests rise, even staunch conservatives opposed to big government clamor for the despised latter to step in and prevent poor Americans from loosing their homes – homes they could not afford and should never have bought in the first place.

Even during such difficult times, however, one can only watch in amazement lines of people camping out in front of department store doors, to be the first ones to rush in at 4 am after Thanksgiving and grab the best "bargains" to add to said toy stash, or to pile up under the Christmas tree in true holiday spirit. And let's not forget, to help suffering retailers to ring up yet another year of record sales.

All of which makes you wonder, whether Jean de La Fontaine's fable "La Cigale et la Fourmi" was ever translated into English, or if it was, why nobody seems to be interested in crickets and ants. Why else would more than 50% of Americans not save but live from paycheck to paycheck, sometimes even needing advances to cover unexpected expenses. And of the workers who do save, 18% borrow from their 401(k) account meant to support them during retirement - as if there truly were no "*übermorgen*".

THE GOOD OLD DAYS

As any young person has heard many times ("young" in this case means adolescent, as opposed to its more benevolent definition, which would include me), the old days were good, in fact golden and much better than the present. Trust me – in reality, this ain't so. One of the causes of this common misrepresentation is how the human mind works. Fortunately, most of us tend to forget negative experiences faster than positive ones; rare exceptions only confirm this rule (My otherwise lovely wife is one of them). I for instance have decided to hate people who deeply hurt me until the end of my days, only to find out that I cannot hold grudges for more than a few days (Well, maybe months).

While this sometimes may prove to be a handicap, as it makes you susceptible to committing the same mistakes again, it proved to be advantageous during the writing of this book. Although it ended up being often critical, I am reasonably certain that it is not just the summary of a grumpy old man whining about the lost past, but the (admittedly sometimes troublesome) nagging of someone never quite satisfied with the status quo.

Yes, things have changed a lot. Rock 'n Roll (in my youth the worst jungle noise my parents could think of) has been replaced with wrap (which I would not call music at all). The world's rainforests are being destroyed at an alarming pace, as are the ocean fisheries, long thought to be inexhaustible. Terrorism is threatening peaceful people everywhere, religions are turning fanatic as in the Dark Ages. Parents can no longer let their children play unsupervised without having to worry about perverts abducting and abusing them. Young people, formerly always slim, trim and beautiful, are now in danger of becoming overweighed and obese.

All of that should not keep you from realizing and appreciating that the present is a fantastic time to experience. Today's science allows us to understand much (though by far not all) about ourselves and the world we live in, technology permits us to visit and experience even remote parts of this beautiful planet. Compare this to the limitations of past generations, when a trip to the Amazon or Antarctic was an incredibly expensive, time-consuming and potentially lethal venture.

So don't listen to the old geezers, but make the best of the great tools you have and enjoy, what former generations have left for you. The future may be bright or not (dependent on how badly we screw it up for you and your children), but the present is definitely terrific, and beats the "good old days" hands down.

THE UNDECIDED

In Europe, election campaigns can take anywhere from a few weeks to several months, plenty of time to familiarize yourself with the candidates and their platforms. Here we have enjoyed (endured) stump speeches, debates and endless analyses for almost two years – and low and behold, there was still a significant segment of undecided voters.

What do these people need to know to make up their mind? We have heard everything from irrelevant details such as the person's middle name (most of us have little influence on how our parents choose to name us) to the more important candidate's bio and – most important – his or her voting record in the past. We know their party affiliation and have seen their choice of running mate, we even know their marital history and religion (both should be private matters and as unimportant as their gender and race).

We have also been told about their plans and priorities. One voted for the Iraq war and planned to win it whatever it would take, the other ("that one") voted against it and wants to end it as soon as possible. One wanted to cut taxes for everyone, including the richest 5 %, the other ("that one" again) wants to lower them only for low and middle income Americans, but raise it for the wealthy few who can afford it. One was pro life, the other one (guess who) pro choice. One wanted to negotiate with the country's enemies only after they had met certain conditions (which is usually the result of negotiations, not a prerequisite), the other one wants to sit down with them unconditionally, but after careful preparations. One is old and showed the wear and tear of a long campaign, the other one in his prime without any known health problems.

What else was there to evaluate for an intelligent decision? Who was still undecided at that point, probably made up his or her mind at the spur of the moment or – for the benefit of the country – did not vote at all.

TOYS

Most adults need toys at least as much as children – the fancier and more expensive the better. Only the best, I am told, allow you (actually, just about guarantee you) to excel at your hobby – but I cannot but wonder.

We had a friend in Germany who cross-country-skied (trail-less, of course) with ancient wooden skis he prepared for the season with pitch. When we happened to encounter an established ski area's black diamond downhill run on the way, he would just for fun telemark it down, leaving the stunned high-tech crowd behind. A coworker of mine was on the side a skiing instructors' instructor for the professionals' annual update. She did this with 10 year-old skis and, the last time I saw her, while 6 months pregnant.

My wife and I go hiking about once every week, usually on very rugged mountain or desert trails. We often get to admire other people's $ 200 boots, while we kind of hide ours ($ 30 or – if we splurged - $ 50) at the trailhead. It has to be there, since we don't see them again on the trail, far away from the parking lot. We have, however, been passed on the way down into Grand Canyon by a woman in Tevas, who obviously did not know any better.

En route to desert hikes in our small SUV, we have gone by impressing-looking vehicles (MSRP more than twice that of ours) standing on top of a drop-off their drivers considered too dangerous. Admittedly, ours has limited slip differential and skid plates (not advertised on its rear end), but boy, did the others look great.

After I gave a slide presentation to the photography club at Princeton University, the first question I was asked, was "What camera do you use?" – the same one I hear, whenever people look at pictures of mine on my website. I guess they would also ask a painter about the make of his brushes.

So believe it or not – while top of the line toys are a blessing for the industry, they don't make great sportsmen or artists. Future baseball stars are still discovered among kids hitting cans with sticks in the streets of Cuba or the Dominican Republic, and shark-skin swimsuits are only essential when you plan to break world records at the Olympics. Short of that, it is not your equipment that is limiting.

TRADITIONS

Every people seems to cherish most what it has least of. Germans rave about the beauty of their country's unspoilt natural areas (few and far between) but take their many centuries old quaint villages for granted, while Americans declare any old shack older than 150 years a National Historic Monument, but don't hesitate to pollute and plunder their vast open back country. Most European nations will raze anything in the way of modern development, unless it is a major architectural treasure many hundred years old, in the US an old cemetery will stop the bulldozers any time. Even arguably ugly industrial or military buildings are deemed worthy of protection, if older than a century (Make that 80 years – just visit Mare Island north of San Francisco).

Similarly, any event that has taken place more than a few times becomes a "time-honored tradition", and items invented by clever marketing people a decade or two ago are now sold at premium prices as "traditional local products" ("Julian Pie" is a good example in our San Diego area). Clever American entrepreneurs even invent foreign traditions to market here. We have seen mail-order catalogs advertise a Christmas tree ornament in the shape of a pickle, "an old German tradition" to delight presumably overjoyed children. Can anybody seriously believe traditional Germans would adorn their festive tree with of all things a green pickle?

Few cultures have held their natural resources and historic traditions in equally high esteem, and those who have were sooner or later overrun by greedy and reckless conquerors. Some of the pre-Columbian civilizations of Central America are well-known examples, but you don't even have to go that far. North America's native people lived off the land but in harmony with the environment, not taking more than they truly needed. They respected nature as much as the spirits of their ancestors, and maintained their traditions like powwows, dances and burial rituals over many generations.

Until those savages were driven from their (wasted, since not fully exploited) homelands and re-educated to appreciate the cultural superiority of the colonizers. They learned about the blessings of alcohol, guns and quick money, and the ubiquitous casinos on Indian reservations are one proof of the program's success, the countless gift stores selling turquoise jewelry and kachina dolls (now more rationally carved from balsa wood) another. If they would finally also subscribe to Halloween and turkey dinners, Native Americans could be called genuinely traditional.

Traffic Rules

Different countries have different rules, and if you travel a lot, it often takes some adjusting to feel comfortable driving the local streets and highways. Most glaringly different of course are those nations requiring you to drive on the wrong, pardon, left side – usually present or former members of the British Commonwealth. Pay particularly close attention there, as some of these countries also have very tough enforcement rules. I still remember New Zealand, where my exceeding the speed limit by 5 mph resulted in a $80 fine and the threat that, if I did not pay up, my car would be impounded and our house might be confiscated (I did not pay, fled that country and am now probably on their Most Wanted list).

A European specialty are traffic circles (called round-abouts in the UK), but to keep the visitor confused, with different national rules. In Germany for instance, you have the right of way once you are circulating, in other countries any car coming into the circle has it (If you are not sure, just behave as if you were in New Jersey, where there are no rules.). Then there are highways with one lane in each direction, plus a center lane than can be used from either to pass or make left turns. That was common in France but never in Germany, where it would have resulted in countless head-on collisions. Four-way-stops, by the way, you also don't see in the latter country, since every driver would try to beat the slow-poke other. Civilized merging has been accepted, however (called the

"*Reißverschluss-System*", the zipper system), although differently from here. When lanes have to merge, drivers wait until they reach the actual bottle-neck instead of clearing the blocked lanes miles before it becomes necessary (You guessed it – I am a "late merger", also called "cheating driver" by the early ones.). And when an on-ramp merges into a freeway, people actually respect the right-of-way of the oncoming fast vehicles instead of pulling into the expressway at 25 mph right in front of them. Usually not a problem here, by the way, since all decent drivers have learnt to drive in the left lanes (see below) – except, of course, for the reckless speeders, who have discovered that the rightmost lane is frequently empty and the fastest.

South of our border, the first thing you notice are the infamous *topes* or "Sleeping Policemen", speed bumps sometimes high and sharp enough to do serious damage to the belly of your car, and occasionally enriched by near-by *vibradores* reminiscent of the washboard sections of car makers' test circuits. What really slows you down more than any artificial road obstacles are the dreaded *doble-remolques* crawling up steep and winding mountain roads of Mexico's interior at top speeds of about 3 mph, usually followed by long lines of other vehicles. Every now and then, one frustrated driver will pull out and pass the behemoth, hilltops and blind curves non-withstanding, and miraculously survive, since any oncoming traffic seems to expect such maneuver and is ready to slam the brakes. Another local custom is best experienced in Mexico City during rush hour (which extends from 5am to 11pm): Don't ever give an inch in multilane intersections and during merges. He who has the best nerves wins and gains at least a full car length, once the unavoidable gridlock will have cleared after a half hour or so. The same rule applies in the Brazilian mountain villages around Rio de Janeiro, normally with even greater success (jams last about 2 hours).

Other Latin American driving customs are well worth keeping in mind, too. In Venezuela's capital Carácas, for instance, red traffic lights at best play the role of Yield signs elsewhere, but often are completely ignored and run at full speed. So practice what you have probably already learnt in your native Maryland or California, and carefully inch into the intersection, once your light has turned green.

Other California traffic rules, by the way, are limited to this state, where every student driver seems to have been taught them from day one. On divided highways, for example, always drive in the leftmost lane, when you don't want to be bothered by traffic entering from on-ramps. That way you can concentrate on your phone conversation, make-up or snacking and don't have to worry about all those maniacs zooming by on your right. Also there is no minimum speed requirement – so you can cruise comfortably and watch the speeders slaloming their way through the other lanes. When you do decide to leave your favorite lane (e.g. to cross over to the exit ramp fifty feet ahead), do as you would in the city and don't touch that turn signal lever. Not signaling your intentions keeps the other drivers alert and adds to overall road safety, as does driving with only your position lights on during heavy rain or fog. City driving in general is not too different from that on freeways: Always stick to the left lane, slow down to no more than 25 mph if you plan to turn left in a few miles, and never forget that using any other lane is a sign of weakness. If you then finally also remember that those octagonal red signs mean to make no more than a polite suggestion (They don't call it a Hollywood Stop for nothing), you should be doing just fine and blend right in.

In general before driving in a different state or country, it pays to watch the locals and try to assimilate their style. For a foreigner, muddling through without an accident might be easiest in the US, where many drivers are considerate and patient, if you are not quite sure what to do at an intersection. In Germany, you would be reminded by honking that you are obstructing traffic; in Mexico City the honking starts the very moment the light turns green. If you like driving fast, however, a few German Autobahns are still the place to go – and the only one where I was ever able to experience 160 mph speeds without breaking the law. No such opportunity here, but avoiding accidents with drivers, who have not yet figured out how to use the rear mirror or turn signals is exhilarating enough. Throw in a few state specialties such as New Jersey's jug handles, and visitors can have almost as much fun driving here as in Paris or the Mediterranean.

TRAVEL

Next to living in a foreign country, traveling is by far the best way to learn to understand other cultures; reading about them helps, but is not enough (nor is seeing Russia from your living room, by the way – even if it were true). Traveling a certain way, that is: If as an American you spend your time abroad in American chain resorts and limit your exposure to the natives to organized sightseeing tours, you are missing the point – just as Germans during a charter trip to Mallorca, where they join their countrymen and –women over beer and bratwurst in a restaurant catering to them (*Hier wird deutsch gesprochen – und gesungen*).

Done the right way, on your own by rail, road or on foot, you will soon find out that people anywhere are friendly, helpful and hospitable, and if you manage to overcome language barriers enough to have meaningful conversations, that they share most of your hopes and concerns. I have never met any real traveler, who did not speak enthusiastically about the places he or she has visited, us included. Whether it was Switzerland or Indonesia, Fiji or Brazil, we always felt like welcome visitors, never only as a cash cow to be milked (which would have been a big disappointment anyway, as we are usually quite barren).

Wherever you go, just make sure to avoid large groups of tourists, in particular your compatriots. Somehow fellow human beings of any nationality manage to become obnoxious when in a horde, and while Americans and Germans are no worse than Swedes, Dutch, French, Italians, etc. (My apologies to Poles and Japanese, but rest assured – you are included), they are bad enough and will spoil your encounter with the locals.

WHAT IF

Friends of ours say they are not going to vote, since all politicians are the same, and whoever wins won't make a difference for the country. Just looking at the last few years already proves them wrong, however.

Take Germany for instance. From being Europe's economic engine, the country had deteriorated to becoming its tail light. Much of the frustrated population was hunkering down and waiting for better times; patriotism was out. Visiting our home country was outright depressing, and we could only share our more optimistic friends' hope for profound change.

Then came Ms. Merkel (a Ph.D. physicochemist) and, due to her narrow election victory, the need for a grand coalition. The partnering parties were forced to bridge their differences, find working compromises and actually got the country moving again. Within a few years, unemployment dropped, consumer spending was up, the economy started to boom again, and Germans were no longer embarrassed to fly their colors. Equally successful was the foreign policy, and straight-talking diplomacy resulted in respect from allies and more distant world powers. The German navy now patrols the waters off the Lebanese coast, and army and air force help to keep peace and reconstruct Afghanistan. This is the role we had always hoped for our home country: Be strong and make use of this strength in peaceful missions around the world.

The United States, on the other hand, was in a different starting position. As the world's only remaining superpower, it could have been the benevolent giant of fairy tales and spread a message of democracy and "compassionate capitalism" throughout the developing world. Then came Mr. Bush (main credentials: a DUI conviction and a bankruptcy), and what could go wrong went wrong. With naïve arrogance, he lectured the world, insulted friends and foes alike, and prided himself of "awe and shock" war-waging rather than generous support of those in need. Instead of bipartisan consensus-building (counterpart to the "Grand Coalition"), this president polarized the country as no one before during our lifetime, immobilizing a less than dynamic bickering Congress. An anticipated substantial budget surplus was turned into a huge deficit (mainly due to an ill-conceived and badly executed "preemptive" war), the booming economy turned sour, the formerly seemingly indestructible greenback became the wobbly Bush Dollar, and the nation leading in environmental issues now hides behind developing countries ("If they don't clean up their act, we won't either"). Torture and Big Brother-type surveillance are sanctioned, since the goal justifies the means, and science and religion have made a giant step – backwards towards the medieval age..

Now imagine, how history would have developed, if Americans had elected a Merkel for president. The country could still be the unchallenged superpower, thousands of American boys and girls and countless Iraqis would be alive, and the Afghan war would have been won instead of largely been delegated to Pashtun tribes of mixed loyalty. Al Quaida and the Taliban would be on the run in the mountains of Pakistan and not be training more terrorists in their newly created safe haven of Iraq's power vacuum. The economy would be humming along (with money to spare to shore up Social Security, fix the infrastructure, search for alternative energies and finally improve the healthcare system), and American travelers would be received world-wide as welcome visitors (Many friends of ours no longer travel abroad – not just because of the Bush economy, but also, since they are afraid of harassment and worse.) I don't think scientists should rule the world – but it would help, if its most powerful leader would understand that climate change is not a myth, and that the "Theory of Evolution" beats Intelligent Design hands-down. And if this president really wanted another war, how about invading Darfur?

While I am deeply sorry for our host country, I am very happy for Germany. If they had ended up with a Bush, the sagging economy would have been my lesser worry. More dangerous would have been a revival of the dark-age mantra *"Am deutschen Wesen soll die Welt genesen"*, which proved to be just as devastating for the world as "There are only two ways of doing things – the American and the wrong way" is now.

The one consolation is that many of these negative developments are not irreversible. It will take a long time and a major effort to restore the world's faith in America, but with the right person at the helm, it will happen. The first step has already been made.

RIGHT OR WRONG – MY COUNTRIES

Now that you have read some of or even this entire book, you may be wondering, whether I am simply a misanthrope whining and complaining just about everything coming my way. The answer is a resounding, "Not at all". I always have enjoyed life at its fullest and still do, from hard work to equally hard play (as the Aussies recommend; I definitely have to visit there), always together with the good people I have found everywhere. And we (my wife of many years included) love the United States as much as Germany and are hard-pressed to answer the question, which country we consider home.

Both, while lovable, however, are far from perfect, and progress is never achieved by complacently applauding the *status quo*. That's why this book was written – not to just nag, but to instigate thought about further improvements (Trust me, American patriot, those are possible.). So compare what you see during your travels (real or armchair) to what you have, and help my two home countries to learn from each other's strengths. This will make sure they stay the best in the world, together with the many others that also are.